T0380945

UN-I-VER-SE
FOR THE
UNIVERSE

Inspired by God, put into words
by Samantha Wilezol

WestBow Press books may be ordered through booksellers or by contacting:

WestBow Press
A Division of Thomas Nelson & Zondervan
1663 Liberty Drive
Bloomington, IN 47403
www.westbowpress.com
844-714-3454

Because of the dynamic nature of the Internet, any web addresses or links contained in this book may have changed since publication and may no longer be valid. The views expressed in this work are solely those of the author and do not necessarily reflect the views of the publisher, and the publisher hereby disclaims any responsibility for them.

Any people depicted in stock imagery provided by Getty Images are models, and such images are being used for illustrative purposes only.
Certain stock imagery © Getty Images.

Scripture taken from the Holy Bible, NEW INTERNATIONAL VERSION®. Copyright © 1973, 1978, 1984, 2011 by Biblica, Inc. All rights reserved worldwide. Used by permission. NEW INTERNATIONAL VERSION® and NIV® are registered trademarks of Biblica, Inc. Use of either trademark for the offering of goods or services requires the prior written consent of Biblica US, Inc.

ISBN: 979-8-3850-2230-4 (sc)
ISBN: 979-8-3850-2231-1 (e)

Library of Congress Control Number: 2024906441

Print information available on the last page.

WestBow Press rev. date: 07/29/2024

WESTBOW
PRESS®
A DIVISION OF THOMAS NELSON
& ZONDERVAN

Verses That Inspired Me To Write This Book For King Jesus:

Philippians 3:13:
"Brothers and sisters, I do not consider myself yet to have taken hold of it. But one thing
I do: Forgetting what is behind and straining toward what is ahead." (NIV Version)

Matthew 24:13-14:
"But the one who stands firm to the end will be saved. [14] And this
gospel of the kingdom will be preached in the whole world as a
testimony to all nations, and then the end will come." (NIV)

John 13:7:
"Jesus replied, "You do not realize now what I am doing, but later you will understand."" (NIV)

Ecclesiastes 6:10-12:
"Whatever exists has already been named, and what humanity is has been
known; no one can contend with someone who is stronger." (NIV)

Ephesians 3:18-19
"...may have power, together with all the Lord's holy people, to grasp how wide and
long and high and deep is the love of Christ, and to know this love that surpasses
knowledge—that you may be filled to the measure of all the fullness of God."(NIV)

Ephesians 3:20:
"Now to him who is able to do immeasurably more than all we ask or
imagine, according to his power that is at work within us." (NIV)

PREFACE:

By Samantha Wilezol

It is easy to want something bigger than ourselves, or to want to become something bigger than ourselves, and the answer is right in front of us. Could it be someone who wants to come live inside of you, for all of the human race?

It is easy to want to try to strive to become something, but who are *you* when you're alone? (not what you do?) Does striving for what you *want* to be actually change who you are as a physiologically made human being? Some may wonder, *Could there be more to life, than what I can tangibly see?*

It's not *What is next in my life?* or *What's the next big thing the world can offer?* Could it be what is already here, that the beginning of time predestined, for *jeez, us?*

There was something different happening in the entire world when at the beginning of time, it was counting backwards instead of upwards. After something came that was predestined would come, then time started counting up, leading into A.C., to now currently A.D. Could the "C" in B.C. in A.C. point to *jeez, us?*

Un-I-Ver-Se For The Universe
Inspired by God, Written Into Words By Samantha Wilezol:

We all just want wholeness and constance in our lives. We may hear ourselves say that we need some space, a break from people and places and things, and the best place to go to that would be space. When we don't understand ourselves or circumstances in life, we see that the formation of the planets, and the things that are giving us light on earth, before the first person was on the earth to formulate ideas, pointed to a circle, universally known as wholeness and constance.

When you're alone, your tie or makeup off for the day, away from expectations, obligations, and demands from the day, and you lay down, hearing your fan softly buzzing, you realize that all of us are not constant. Our bodies are all getting older, day by day, something we can't get away from.

What could be constance? The world is always changing. People are always changing, standards of what you have to do in religious customs are always changing. Education requirements, expectations in relationships, and expectations on ourselves are also always changing. It can even be hard to find happiness in the world or in people because they're always changing, too.

"O" sounds like "a choo", what we say when we sneeze. Could the shape of the planets and the shape that things grow out from, like flowers, be the one who is perfect and constant, who wants to save our lives? And similar to bacteria that is being seen (through a circle lens), whether or not it knows it, could it be we are being seen from above from a lens above the Universe, that is also circular, like that of the orbit of the planets' orbit shape? After all, we are so small in this whole Universe, like bacteria. Every "I", like how an "I" is in "UnIverse", has an eye. Could it be from someONE, who has an eye? Could this "I" have a breath?

Your heart skipped a beat when you sneezed. A force interceded on your behalf to have you still be alive. It couldn't have been the person next to you. The force went to your heart. Studies show that your chest lights up when you feel that of a *positive* emotion, primarily being love. What could be the only higher power who is love that gave you a second chance? That gave you a breath when you couldn't breathe? This is not a silly analogy, because you are still alive and breathing, and the average person, within 365 days, sneezes 450 times, 450 times you could have lost your life.

We don't have to do or say anything to see, or to get a second breath when we sneeze. "Se" meaning "he" is at the end of the "universe" . Could it be this I and breath is a he? Who sees *jeez-us*! Wait, that sounds like Jesus.

*Note for the readers: Spanish is the most communicated language in the world, that uses letters that are also used in English, in addition to 99 other languages, that are utilized by the total of individuals accumulating to two *billion*.

Maybe our interpretations are what caused wars viewing the Universe as "dos versus" instead of how it was to be in the beginning, the "Universe". We've been trying to live in a way the "I" of the Universe didn't intend, and that's why we're stressed. If it was called "dos versus", then humans' strive for living as survival of the fittest for humans of being "versus" the other, trying to be better than the other person or climb the ladder of status to the tippy tippy top, would bring us actual joy, not more strife, war, division, mistrust, confusion, and disorder. Also, if the Universe was called "dos versus", it would mean there wouldn't be just One True Overseer. Could it be that the word *Universe* in itself points to how there is only One overseer for all, like "Un" in Universal, and "AI" pointing to for *all.*

You may think, "Hold on. I had a bad experience with church", but maybe we are miscommunicating it like whisper down the lane. We can't have wars without human brains, so maybe we should adjust our interpretations so we can be in align with the truth. You see, a war or conflict can't happen with just one person. No one can argue that a war or argument couldn't have started between two or more people. Initially, the war conflict was started inside of the one person. A war going on inside of the one person led to a war between another person. When we let God settle the spiritual battle in us individually, we'll see there is no more flesh and bone to fight; Just a spiritual battle that Jesus has already won, who is our sword for us, the Sword of the Spirit.

You may find yourself saying, "I want someone to walk in my shoes, no, to actually get under my skin and be of me for a day to understand my failing business, or my struggling kid, or this seemingly impossible class I'm trying to get through. I'm willing to stand under to understand, for them to get under my skin."

*Jesus: Je-sus : sounds like jeez, us: He is "of us"

*Bible: "El Bi-b-le": meaning the same as "Le Bi-b-le": "He-to-b-you" (so that) "You-to-b-He"

*Bible sounds like "viv-le" pronounced in Spanish, "viv le" meaning "live he" (Jesus)

*Side note: When you want to know what a word means, you go to the root of the word in itself. As mentioned, Spanish is the most communicated language in the world, that uses letters that are also used in English, in addition to 99 other languages, that are utilized by the total of individuals accumulating to two *billion*.

Could it be we are the ones who have been twisting it to how we *wanted* it to be? Wait, so you're saying just to be alive and to feel the pain of life can mean the start to know him? Just like how I need four things to live (air, water, food, and sunlight) points to the One who is those four things, who walked in my skin (Jesus, the Breath of Life (John 20:22), Jesus, the Living Water (John 4:14), Jesus, the Bread of Life (John 6:35), and Jesus, the Light of the World (John 8:12), all pointing to verses from the Holy Bible.

Also, I now see how the Bible (in Spanish pronounced as "bee bley") is of my vive (also pronounced in Spanish as "bee bley", the "e" pronounced in Spanish sounding like a "y" when pronounced) that just wants to relate to me. And since this Jesus is proven to be of my Bible (bee blay), I can say "Viv le" ("le" meaning he), live He, now in me. So this "he" is also an "it", like how "el" also means "el" in Spanish, pointing to how El Bible (El Bi-b-le) is he to be you (He-to-b-you) and you to be him (You-to-b-him).. How do I know that? The four things you need are the four things that He is.

So maybe I was wrong about my view on Jesus and the Bible. Maybe the risen cross just wants to cross roads with me, and be and relate to me. Because if the world and Universe was about doing, it would be called the "Uni hace" ("hace" meaning do), and if it was about obtaining more possessions, it would be called the "Uni have". but no, it is called the Universe (Un-I-ver-se) meaning One-I-to-see-He (Jesus).

To see (or ver), we don't have to do anything. Just believe. In Him (se), Jesus.

And all, we are called human *beings*, "ing" showing a work in progress, in that we are not perfect. Also, this world's definition of "perfect" is always changing, so what could be *the* definition of perfect, for all? It has to be the One who is, *heh, of yours (Je-sus), before you and I even existed. Jesus. Absolutely.

*I see now!

So now I see, so I want to believe; *Believe* meaning to "be alive" to believe, to then leave (be-leave) (to Heaven through believing in Jesus), showing this life is not my own. After all, when you pass, you lose weight, proof that your soul leaves your body.

You see, since faith is the cure for believing that something like wind exists, though we have never seen it, I see why I don't need human reasoning for validation that God exists; but rather to experience it, the one who experienced it first and controls it and made it (Jesus). Because when I first believe, then I can see, and to see the effects it has.

To understand, we have to stand under to see things for how they are, helping us to understand through the lens of faith, like using binoculars to see things through a magnified view.

I think it's interesting, too, how we are unconsciously making room for the Supernatural when we turn our clocks back around Christmas, like how when time counted down before Jesus was born, and when we turn our clocks ahead around Easter, pointing to when He will come back to earth. (The supernatural is the super just wanting to meet our natural).

What was CONstant, the constancy of the orbit of the planets pointing to the perfect love of God, came to provide the CONnection so we could be with ("con" in Spanish meaning with) in right-standing with God, through sending Jesus, God in human form, who is of, once again, *jeez, us!*

You were made in God's image (see Romans 8:29). It's just you don't remember. Just because you don't remember doesn't mean it didn't happen. You didn't know it because you couldn't see yourself in your mother's womb, but someone made us who could. God is telling you right now, because he knows you will be ready to receive him, and he will help you to understand. We don't have to remember to *experience* it. Experience helps you to remember (reading the Word of God). Similarly, when people with dementia listen to old-time music, it helps them to remember an old time in their life. Likewise, sin was the dementia that separated us from God, sin meaning "without" in Spanish. But when we hear the Word, Jesus (t) intercedes so it can reach our heart. (**Hear** - "t" coming through (the risen cross of Jesus, represented through "t" interceding) - **heart** ("t" of the cross reaches our heart, after we hear).

Part 2: An Artistc Approach To Aid In Our Understanding:

The ultimate Son, (not the sol, not the sun) has given you, for your soul, this 24 hours, to ask yourself if you are willing to receive Jesus, who is for *jeez, us*, who is of, heh, you (Je-sus), who has revealed himself to all so clearly more than anyone could ask. After all, all the planets orbit around the sun, and no force can cease them from doing so, except for His love, ultimately orbiting around *the* Son (Jesus). Time didn't run out on you, you make time for what's important to you. We all get 24 hours per day.

Staring at the face of a clock can help us become accustomed to staring towards the face of Jesus, who had 12 disciples. We all get an equal opportunity to receive the face of Jesus, and we see proof that God is indeed, the beginning and the end (12am and 12pm). Also, 12 months, or mezas ("mezas" meaning months in Spanish) in a year point to the 12 disciples that was with the table, or "mesa", in Spanish, with Jesus (Luke 22:14-20).

If knowing Jesus personally was about doing, like how religion is associated with doing works and customs, Jesus would not have had bad experiences with religious people, like how he was mocked and persecuted from the *religious* leaders. Knowing Jesus is about a relationship (see Ephesians 2:8-9) hence the name, "Un i VER se" (One I to SEE, He (Jesus), and "con" meaning "with" in the CONstant circle of the shape of the orbit of the planets).

Similar to how he related with the tax collector and woman at the well, He can relate to your struggling business, or being a student struggling in that one class. Even if there's a part of the Bible, hard to understand, we need to remind ourselves to stand under (His sovereignty) to understand, through the lens of faith. When you receive Him, the risen crucifix, it can fix your view on life, and even the hard parts of it. As a matter of fact, *o* in "o'clock" points to how our lives were intended to live for his "o" infinite, agape love, going back to the shape of the planets (a "o" circle) mentioned from the beginning, not to be lived for us (not called iclock). This "o" circle of wholeness, infinity, constance, and perfection points to, who else could it be, but the whole, infinite, constant, perfect love of God, the shape that all of life grows out from too, like flowers.

That even if we try to make a way of how we want the Universe and world to grow, it doesn't change the way it was since the beginning of time, that, as previously mentioned, time first counting backwards in years. You see, there is an *iMessage* for the world from the *iCloud*. Time first counting backwards would point to and predestine what was to become uploaded (The year of BC leading up to Christ being born), so that time is now counting up to what will be downloaded (His return to earth for us to hear from his ear, from our degree (th) of his earth (ear-th).

We now live in AD, the year of our Lord. All of history points to His story, which is the High story, why man's attempt to rule didn't and doesn't work. And that the four corners of this world (North, South, East, and West) foretold, forever, of the four corners of the cross, that the Son rises on. Wherever you try to run or hide from him or yourself in this whole world, you can't outrun the risen cross of Jesus.

It's Interesting how the first and last letter of the Greek language, the language of scientific translatation, of Alpha and Omega, points to how God is the Alpha and the Omega, pointing to Revelation 21:6.

Also, all of direction in the Universe (past, present, and future) points to how God is the same yesterday, today, and forever; In addition to how *1 in math relates to how we are all of one ("of" also meaning multiplication in math) and is the one underliner of everything (like /1, in math), the "Un" in Universe.

You see, if Jesus wasn't the Bread, Breath, Light, and Air for all man (these four things), then I wouldn't need food, air, light, and water in this body. If I didn't need God, I would be able to save myself, but I can't. If I didn't need saving, then a Savior wouldn't have had to come. He is for *jeez, us!* If a Savior didn't have to come, then time wouldn't have been counting backwards in the beginning, pre-destining when He would come, so now that time is now counting up to when he will return. If I was able to save myself, or if there weren't problems, people wouldn't be caught up in numbing their minds towards the problems of the world.

God, the Great I Am, the *Un* and *I* of the Universe saw you before you could see him. So we don't have to skeptize on the unknown anymore, because we were not known before we could know. Just let the unknown make itself known to you through faith, which is to trust to become entrusted to have the unknown make itself known to you, so that you may be shown the secrets of His universe and be given the key to heaven. The supernatural is the super just wanting to meet your natural. Let it meet yours.

So, my friends, revisit the Redeemer to see how you were intended to deem (think) (that affects how you live). If you're saying you're not alive, you're saying Jesus isn't real, because he is, and was these four things, listed, in Himself before you even existed that you are now. And if you're saying you're not alive, you're saying the Bible isn't real, because to be alive is to "vive" (Bi-ble) (Bib-le to vive-El, who is the four things that you are). Then you can reach the recognition of hey, the molecule that holds everything together in my body called Laminin points to the risen cross of Jesus, in that it has the same number of corners as the risen cross of Jesus.

And so, God is the same breath that is of you for Christ followers (realizing it now!), referring to Genesis 2:7, the One we evolved from, not how the world's worldly view thinks we evolved (false evolution) which is apart from The Truth.

Also, the Gospel is gos"pill" to the sure script of the script"sure"s, pres"scripting" what we would face in this world. And everything that is, has, and will happen in the world points to it, including the war in Israel having been predestined to happen in Zechariah chapter 14, and farmers replanting again in Samaria, about 2,000 years later, in which recently happened in which the Bible predestined, in Jeremiah 31:5. Moreover, when you read a verse, it's to see He (ver se).

Verse: ver-se: To see He

And so you see, friends, when you sneezed, referring back to earlier, God was the one who gave you a second chance, whether or not you wanted it, thought you were worthy of it, were too good for it, understood about it, or needed it. You didn't have to say or do anything to be extended it, proof that we don't have to work our way towards heaven, or God's approval. You were given a second chance for what? Maybe to experience the breadth of the Breath that gave you a second breath, before you breathe your last breath, so you know where you'll breathe your first breath after you pass.

Wait so you're saying that God is love? That the message from the Universe is saying we can rest in seeing him (VER in Universe (to see) and SE in Universe (He), that He came so He could Be you (El Bi-b-le : He-to-b-you) so we would want to be Him (Le Bi-b-el : You-to-b-Him). And that to be is intended for us to believe, so we may "be leave" (be brought up to heaven in his timing). That just like how God's love is constant, infinite, and whole, when people of all continents, of North America, South America, Europe, Asia, Australia, and Antarctica, look at the shape of the planets' orbit of the constant, infinite, whole circle of God, we will be able to say, "Sí, I go see Him!" (c-ir-c-le).

So maybe this shows you that when you're alone at the end of the day, whether you're a teacher, pastor, student, "one still trying to figure it all out", and so forth, and you're staring up at the ceiling, hearing your fan buzzing, hearing your soft breathing, you now see that you were already met by Him. It is now time to meet with Him. When we looked in the mirror, we saw we were… mere. But in Christ, we are now a miracle in Him (M-ir-a-c-le : mhm-I-go-to-see-Him, (Spanish view). Friends, *let* Him find you before He finds you out, before it's too late, so you can meet him face-to-face, which was like staring at the face of a clock from all your days, who had 12 disciples, and wants to be yours.

After all, we were unknown and couldn't know during the unknown, so the Bible is for us to simply trust. Once again, just allow the unknown make itself known to you through faith, which is to trust to become entrusted to have the unknown make itself known to you, so that you may be revealed the secrets of His universe and be given the key to heaven. The supernatural is the super just desiring to meet your natural. Let it meet yours.

So what is the message of the Universe for all? When you want to know what a word means, you go to the root of it. The Un-I-ver-se, translated, is One I to see, He (Jesus). You now see that the "Un" and "I" of the Universe (Un-I-VER-se) is the Great I Am, King Jesus, who *is* enough so that we don't have to strive towards being enough. Through all the striving that humans do on earth, some say when they reach their deathbed "I still feel like I don't know who I am." Friend, that doesn't have to be you anymore, because you now see through what the Bible means, once again, that He came to be you so that you would want to be like him, and now you can say "Sí, I go see Him!" (C-Ir-c-le). We can see it relates to Isaiah 40:21-23 in the Holy Bible. Because to be alive is intended for us to believe "be leave" (to heaven). So once again, why don't we revisit the Redeemer to see how we were intended to deem (live) since this beginning. Because Jesus is for *jeez, us!*

(Cease behind the sneeze!): If you sneeze in the morning and blow your nose in a tissue when you wake up, you'll see him dancing the boogie for you in your tissue. That's how much he loves you. He loves you because he loves you. He sees you because he sees you. He wants you because he wants you, the purest love of all time. He is *profoundly* in love towards you, as His child. He just wants you to love Him back. He wants to celebrate the high of highs of life with you and comfort you during the low of lows of life, to *relate* and *feel* life with us. He knows your pain. He knows your name. He wants to comfort you and deliver you from those thoughts you may think at night that you haven't told anyone about, that no human counselor was able to help you out of. He knows what it feels like to have people talk behind your back, your reputation falsely lied about from others, to feel betrayed, to struggle in being in a certain circumstance of life, and so forth; But He also knows what it feels like to be resurrected. Likewise, just like He ascended after He rose from the grave, we will ascend to be with Him after our time on earth. Just believe Him in faith.

So what's the Uni Verse for the Universe? John 3:16: "For God so loved the world that he gave his only Son, that whoever believes in him shall not perish, but eternal life." (Verse, ver-se, "to see He".)

And putting that into action, "If you confess with your mouth that Jesus is Lord, and believe in your heart that God raised Him from the dead, you will be saved" (Romans 10:9).

Matthew 16:24 talks about considering the cost of following Him. When we receive Jesus, we become equipped to follow Him. Just place yourself in a posture of surrender, because He was and is the four things that we need (The Air, Light, Bread of Life, and Breathe of Life), as previously mentioned, before we even existed! Just believe it in faith now.

Realize we were all born holey, so we could become holy in Him, to become wholly in Him. Once again, because if we knew how to be "perfect", the world's definition of it wouldn't always be changing. We were without (sin meaning "without" in Spanish) capability of being "perfect", born with sin. An acronym to remember this is "cheese", "jeez" (Jesus is for jeez, us!), and "keys" (the keys to heaven, we are given!)

This concept of giving our lives to Jesus is not as scary as it seems. In order to purify water, a process called *Reverse Osmosis* is done, which is molecules going from a place of more high concentration to an area that is significantly less high. We now see that it makes sense to how strength humbled itself to becoming feebleness (Jesus coming to earth) so that feebleness (us, mere human beings) could become elevated to being strong, in Him, that purifies us. Jesus is King!

So, once again, what is the Un-I-Ver-Se of the Universe? One-"I"-to-see-He (Jesus), who is of *jeez, us!*

John 3:16: "For God so loved the world that he gave his only Son, that whoever believes in him shall not perish, but eternal life." (Verse, ver-se, "to see He".)

Un-I-Ver-Se: A Holy Revelation

Also by Samantha Wilezol, within this book

Un- Be *un*done (surrendered) to be shown the unknown,

who wants to make Himself known to you (King Jesus)

I- The Great *I* Am (God)

Ver- Believing is seeing (Jesus) (*ver* means to see)

Se- The words "love" and "Dios" looked at more closely, broken down, point to

how God is a He (of the Trinity, who came to earth in flesh form, Jesus).

Jesus is King.

(See the elaboration of the word "love" broken down in ""All Four One" Jesus is a Living Fact" on the next page in this book).

And that, my friends, is the Un-I-ver-se for the Universe.

Extra thought for the readers:
By Samantha Wilezol

We all give up control before we go to sleep at night, and do so in the dark and when we're alone, in which some people are afraid to be alone, or in an invisible environment; As that being said, why are we afraid to give up control to God in the light and around other people? Also, giving up control helps us to feel refreshed for the next day (like giving up control before going to sleep), so giving up of ourselves for God is not a scary thing, but rather something that refreshes our souls!

Also, French origins got the revelation from the Lord to call the word "Universe", the "Universe". They had to have named it after what they saw, how flowers growing in an outward, circular shape that the first humans recognized on earth before any deep human bias, points, to what else, but the whole, constant love of God.

As follows, someone named Bede, a historian of that of English, was the one who got revelation from the Lord to decide to input the name "BC", when time was counting backwards. Christ certainly came to become amongst the common people, you and I, to save them. God gives revelations to "average, ordinary Joe's" for His glory, like how he changed the hearts of people in the Bible. The definition of "Christ" when researched, the "C" in "BC", is the anointed and chosen one, and straight up says it is Jesus of Nazareth. It is not biased to think that Jesus is the Christ, because He is! When you research "who was referred to as the chosen one?", Jesus comes up. No one else was born in the year of "Four" who said they were the chosen or anointed one.

Proof that Jesus Christ is the One (1) to see, He (Uni-ver-se).

The chosen One, and anointed One, Jesus has chosen and anointed you. Just believe it, and receive it in faith.

So in your life, if your numbers are going down in your grades, in your bank account, or your health status, know the One who is in control behind it, in which time was counting down that awaited him, that is now counting up to when he will return.

"All Four One": Jesus is a Living Fact
By Samantha Wilezol

In the year before someone was born, the birth was predestined would be born.

No other thing or person was predestined to come, except for the One who did.

The one who is of *Jeez, us* (wait that sounds like someone), points to science and science points to Him/it. Science is taught in schools though Scientology isn't forced, so the One of *jeez, us*, can be taught in schools because it is a fact, living after all, and people have the choice to believe in it if they feel led to (you will never regret following Jesus Christ!)

Some back up information on this is how the year He was born points to how He is the One of the four things that we need (readers, read John 6:35, John 8:25, John 20:21-22, John 7:37-39, and John 8:12, referring to how Jesus is the air, bread, breath, and light of the world (four elements humans need to survive, but all found in the One, Him). Science points to Him and he points to science. He claimed to be the chosen One and is. Jesus is a fact (living!) Hebrew names in early years had meaning. Jesus: *jeez, [is for] us!*

Why else would have time dramatically changed with the one who said he was the anointed one who was, has came, and how time didn't dramatically change when other people said in different eras that they were the one (they were not). Jesus Christ is the only true King!

It was unknown to say you were the chosen one "b4" (before) the one who did, proof He came from the unknown, to then make himself known, to be known, to choose us. Because anything of one {*1} is itself, like if you picture the parabola being a reflection at line "One" or "Four" (see my picture in this book included).

We are of it/He, and it/He is of us. *El* means *el.. he* and *it.* The parabola "mirror" proves it.

Also, it is proven that God is love through revelation given to me by God, in that when you say "love", it sounds like "of". "Of" in Spanish is "de". We all know love is of us, so when you add "os" after "de", it forms the word "Dios", meaning God in Spanish, the 2nd most spoken language, that uses English letters, in the world. That is proof, friends, that *love* in itself points to God.

Note: Mythology: *myth i*n the word means *fake*, and shows such as *Star Wars* are fiction

Part Two: By Samantha Wilezol

The Higher Power that is most popular in this country, and is the only true Higher Power, is the only ruler who was the first one to say for Himself that he *was* the Chosen One, who has a letter "O" in it, pointing to the "o" orbit shape of the planets (say "oh!" to the "O").

Trust To Become Entrusted
By Samantha Wilezol

The Bible is holy, so it is to trust, not fully understand. When we trust, we become entrusted to be shown what was once the unknown, to be shown the secrets of the Universe and be given the key to heaven through Jesus Christ!

3,2,1, Happy New Year!
By Samantha Wilezol
We count down before a new year, before a rocket takes off, and to await
food ready in a microwave, to await something new, similar to how time was
counting down to await something new that would come, that did!

***So what does Jesus want to be in my life?

Since we now see that the Bible is real, once again, if knowing God was about rule keeping, then Jesus would not have been persecuted by the *religious* leaders (Matthew 21:23). Also, Isaiah 64:6 talks of how our good works are like dirty rags apart from Him. Jesus came to relate and feel with us, and that we can live for Him through a posture of surrender. It's interesting to see that the shortest verse in the Bible is "Jesus wept", and He never sinned (John 11:35).

NEXT STEPS FOR NEW BELIEVERS:

As Christ followers, all our sins washed away (past, present, and future, by Jesus) our purpose on earth is to now continue to love on God and share His love with others (Mark 12:30-31), and become more like Jesus through sanctification in a posture of surrender (1 Thessalonians 4:3), through the renewing of our minds in His Word, until He calls us home to heaven (Revelation 21:1-4).

*Get plugged into a Christ-centered church and in community with other Christ followers!

God bless!

For readers going through a hard time:

You may think, "That sounds great and all, but you don't know my situation, you don't know what I've done, or I am new to believing in this." I would like to kindly say to you, that God is the God of Israel, so is real (Israel, is real), so is meant to be experienced as real in your life, no matter what you are going through. And in Christ, you receive a new mind. I would also encourage you, once again, in Christ Jesus, to succumb (give up) your stance towards your circumstances to the circumference of God's unfailing, agape love for you. Because He experienced what you are experiencing.

Extra cool thoughts for the readers:
All by Samantha Wilezol, inspired by God, as well:

I want to thank my good brother in Christ for sharing with me and posting the verse specifically that points to God's agape love circle! (Isaiah 40:22)

How To Reach People Of All Ages With Reference to the Higher Power (God!):
By Samantha Wilezol

- For boys: say "hi" to the Higher Power for more more "pow" in your life!

- For teens: for a lasting high, go to the Higher Power that is not a temporary high.

- For little girls: go to the High-Power to be called "your highness" by Jesus!

- For adults: Let God fax the facts to your heart, and a change of root yields a change of fruit.

- For people who like history: history points to His story, and the High story. Let God fax the facts to your heart.

- For people who like science: we are the four things that Jesus is (John 6:35, John 4:14, John 20:22 8:12 and bonus (#5), shelter (God is our shelter)! (John 15:4-5).

- For people who like math: *1 and /1 - We are of ("of" like multiple) One (God) and God is the underliner of everything (the common denominator of one)

- For people who like writing and language, translations and reading: Greek language points to how God is the Alpha and the Omega, and the first VERtebraes, fish, are translated to what Jesus is (Ichthys) (each of the letters in the Greek word points to God), that turned into the now Christian fish sign; Proof the start of the universe points to Jesus.

- For people who like politics, or intrigued by the founding of our country:

We wonder why our kids are not as well-behaved, and it is because the Bibles were taken out of school.

A war or conflict can't happen with just one person. No one can argue that a war or argument couldn't have started between two or more people. Initially, the war conflict was started inside of the one person. A war going on inside of the one person led to a war between another person. When we let God settle the spiritual battle in us individually, we'll see there is no more flesh and bone to fight; Just a spiritual battle that Jesus has already won, who is our sword for us, the Sword of the Spirit.

Outer anger points to inner anger in the one individual. Some may feel anger towards religion because their view on it is wrong, thinking it's on what you do (proof that there will be no more flesh and bone left to fight, proof that our wrong *interpretations* can cause conflict). Anger can be a spirit, sadly. People may sadly say "I have a spirit of anger", to just hold up the sword of the spirit is incredible freedom in Christ, the spirit of His freedom!

For Spanish speakers or bilingual individuals like myself, all glory to God:

Buenos dias points to how every day is a good day. "Dios" (God) sounds like "dias". God is always good despite our circumstances, similar to how we always say *buenos dias* and *buenos tardes,* or *good morning* and *good afternoon,* despite our circumstances.

For people who like Santa Clause: (see proposals section)

People who like poetry: His grace is for all the human race. His love came from above, like a dove, so that to be made free is to live in His love. (Original poem of mine for Christ)

For people who like to see through drawings: (See my drawings for Christ section)

For lovers of math (God bless you if you do!):

The one of the universe is of everything (*1)
Sine (sin) pointed to the opposite of who we were created to be (opposite over hypotenuse: (hypotenuse as the high-lengthed side, like the Higher power)
The sin divided us of ourselves (12/1 / 12/1)
To bring us back to the One, as a solution to the problem, the opposite had to take on itself and make it of itself.
(12/1 * 1/12 = 1).
We are now made right with him through believing in Him in faith.

WAYS TO HELP TEACH DIFFERENT PEOPLE OF DIFFERENT THOUGHT PROCESSES HOW WE WERE SEPARATED FROM GOD, BUT HOW HE MADE A WAY THROUGH CHRIST:

For the intellectual minded (earTH) ("TH" representing a degree of a concept):

Sneeze anaology (see main writing below for elaboration): we were separated from God.

His breath: he gave us saving.

When people drown, you can accept the saving or not. Make the right decision in gratefully receiving it, confessing your sins to Him to receive His grace!

When you pass, your soul leaves your body, proof heaven is real.

We are not called human "doings", we are called human "beings", to be in the image of God.

For the artsy minded (eARTh):

Sin: without God of days (Dios, Dias) (sin means "without" in Spanish)

Sin was the amnesia that separated us from remembering we were made in the image of God. When we hear God's Word, that is similar to wearing headphones that helps us to remember when we were made in God's image, like when older people hear old music through headphones to help them remember an older time in their life.

Repent of your sins and believe in Him, to then leave (to heaven) with Him!

For those with sensitive heart strings: (EARth):

What if I told you there was a love predestined to come after you?

In the analogy of relating it to a spouse, you may have doubted it when someone told you before you met them, but once you got to know them, the previous doubt is now drowned out in love.

If you were the only person on the Earth, Jesus would still come to die for you. Also, He went to the cross, even though He may have not *felt* like it (experiencing a very painful thing), but He knew it had to be done. He could have gotten down at any point, but He didn't. His love is what kept Him there for you.

He lived 33 years of a sinless life. He didn't say one cuss word when he was hanging on the cross for 2 to 3 hours. We may have accidentally heard a cuss word come out of our mouth in the past if we stubbed our toe.

God's Word, the Bible, is His love letter and His love story to you from the holy eternal realm in heaven.

God doesn't need us, but He wants us anyway, simply because He loves us unconditionally. Just confess your sins to Him and receive Him in faith.

Note to the readers before reading this section:

As you read, refer to the key below to think of which section each paragraph can fit into!

Key:

1. Sounds: we sounded out words before we could understand words. Wait what? Yeah. Sounds familiar? Because it is. The soundness of sounds. (Hear.. t.. heart.. See Jesus)
2. Words: Oh word, we can now take The Word's word for it.
3. Shapes: we learned with shape blocks when we were babies to make sense of things.
4. Science: Some people say science helps us to understand life. Well, let's let it help us to understand, well, life (With the exception of false beliefs like evolution)
5. Math: Some people say math helps us to understand life. Well, let's let it help us to understand, well, life (with the exception of false beliefs like the Big Bang)
6. Places: Some people say places bring them back to a certain time in their life, even if you don't remember it without being there. To remember is to simply be a member again (in Him). Your membership never expires in Him. One time surrendered to, good for a lifetime!
7. Drawings- (circle) Even the first caveman drew before he could talk. Drawing things God shows you is simply, well, drawing of what you see, like the circular shape of the planets). Notice that the world apart from God sadly adds human bias when they explain things of worldly ideas. But remember in Christ, that we are set apart!

Extra cool thoughts for the readers:
All inspired by God, put in words by Samantha Wilezol:

When "le" looks in the mirror, it sees "el". When you (el) look in the mirror, you can see He (el), in you! On an applicable, visual standpoint, if you wear a shirt that says "le" on it, when you physically look in the mirror, it says "el". He sees you so you can see Him, so you will want to be like Him, who became flesh before you did, setting an example, helping us to navigate through life, "el vive", pointing to el Bible.

More than half of the Bible are Psalms, that point to relating with Jesus. Jesus came into this world to RELATE with us. A walk with Jesus is not about mere rule keeping. Even the King didn't wear a ring, and a cry even came from the Christ. Jesus knew what it felt like to be single all His life and have people sadly turn their back towards Him.

If you're tempted to compare yourself to others and think, "Why am I not at that same stage of my life as them?", trust the One who is orchestrating it!

You may have certain thoughts at night you may not tell anyone about, but that God knows and wants to heal you from.

Some people are afraid of being alone with their thoughts, or taking a break from the hustle and bustle lifestyle, of working alot or going out a lot, because some may wonder, "If I actually get alone with my thoughts, what will I find?" There can be an anchor for our thoughts, if our thoughts seem that order, or if we don't know where to begin in our minds, and His Name is Jesus Christ, of *jeez, us*! He also knows all of our thoughts even before we think them, pointing to Psalm 139:2.

All answers of the world that people are trying to look for at a library are found in one thing, the Bible (Biblio-techa). God orchestrated it that when you were at the library for a long time trying to find an answer to that one thing, he was trying to get your attention when you saw the name of the place that you were at, that the answer is found in Him, the Bibliotecha the Bibio (Bible) (sounds like Biblia) techa (shelf) (the One book on the shelf). Also, the word "bibliography" points to how our lives should be lived out and according to the Bible (Biblio : Bible : sounds like Biblia)

When we look through the lens of what sees us to view how we see ourselves (God), no human instrument can measure that.

We try to measure things through human instruments to try and make sense of things, but if we were to give up trying to understand the unknown, the unknown would speak for itself. We want to try to understand things and try to, but we honestly don't. Humans don't know what they're doing apart from God, and that's why Jesus had to come!

We say "Bruenos Dias" and "Buenos Tardes" to every day, whether or not the day's circumstances appear to be good or not. "Dias" sounds like "Dios", "Dios" meaning "God", how God is of all days. When you look at the word "good" like in good morning or good afternoon, you see that the word God is in it with the agape love of God circle "o" in it too (God, good). This points to how God is good every day, despite the world's circumstances. Once again, let's just succumb our stance towards our circumstances towards the circumference of God's unfailing, agape love; To see things through the lens of how he sees it, not through how we used to see it.

Be undone to be shown the unknown to know it through the lens of faith.

Don't let yourself hit rock bottom before realizing that the resurrected rock can rock your world!

The earth has 3 parts, the Core, Crust, and Mantle, like how the Trinity is three in one.

An egg has 3 parts, the yolk, shell, and white, and there's 12 eggs in a dozen, the One who made the 12 months in a year.

God's love is keeping all the planets afloat, and has the sun not move any closer or further away from the earth, so we wouldn't freeze or the opposite.

Let our air show we are an heir to someone.

A graduation cap has four sides, like the risen cross of Jesus. We have graduated from the old testament elementary school rules, to graduate into HIGH school so we could see the HIGHer power to then see his message for the Universe (Un-I-ver-se) (One-I-to-see-He (Jesus))

Take the "i" out of *life*, and we will see *love*. God's love.

The Bible has a thesis. Read it for its thesis to understand the whole message, pointing to Christ.

When Jesus was the founding of the country, no wonder things seemed more in order.

To trust Jesus is to become entrusted to be revealed the secrets of the Universe and keys to heaven.

The "g" in past false godz points to the one true, capital *G* God.

The *imessage* for you has come from the *icloud* from God. Jesus has been uploaded (born) into the world so He can be downloaded into your heart.

Message for the ciudad: ci ur dad: See your Dad (your Heavenly Father)

Wow, Laminin looks like the shape of the risen cross of Jesus, the molecule that holds our whole body together.

The shape of the cross looks like a bird's eye view of an airplane, pointing to the Great Comission that Jesus calls us to for Him!

Fish were the first vertebrates on the earth, the Greek word for *fish* pointing to Jesus, each letter in ichthys pointing to that of Jesus Christ (the word of ichthys), that then turned into the Christian fish sign.

Jumping on a trampoline is like a Christ followers' walk with Jesus. When we think we're falling down in circumstances, Jesus' grace helps us to bounce back up.

It's not "Are you, Baptist, Lutheran, Protestant, or Non Denominational, it's are you a follower of Jesus Christ? Yes!"

It is the love of God keeping all the continents afloat, in the midst of all the tsunami, earthquakes, and changes in temperature.

Let the agape love of God "ball" (the circle shape of the planets is the same shape of a ball) (Isaiah 40:21-23) remind you to let God lead your every step (the ball of your foot); So that you may recognize him in everything you do, like how the ball of a sport points to his agape love (soccer ball, basketball, basketball hoop, tennis ball, etc), a hoola hoop, the circular wheels under a rollerskate, the steering wheel and wheels of a car, the circles shape of a tutu, and so forth.

Just like how a ship needs the right amount of wind and rudder to move forward, let your Christian walk be a healthy balance of spirit and truth. Too much spirit is liberalism, which could lead to being emotion lead, and too much truth is legalism (we are not under rules anymore).

It's not "Are you Republican or Democrat? Are you team Jesus, teaming up with His love and grace!"

The word *holiday* has from the Greek word meaning *holy day*. Also, *Christ* is in Christmas (more of Christ).

See link to my Biblical interpretation of the word *newspaper:*

https://docs.google.com/document/d/1HfS6gxlAfH6ZMp9t UeeCYauMhV4nXhcneqeqpuskVA/edit?usp=sharing

See same link to how the risen cross of Christ points to direction and time:

https://docs.google.com/document/d/1HfS6gxlAfH6ZMp9t UeeCYauMhV4nXhcneqeqpuskVA/edit?usp=sharing

Isaiah 40:21-23 points to there's a lens in heaven, the eyes of God. Every lens has an eye, like a camera. The circle shape of the orbit of the planets points to God always watching over us. Bacteria is being seen through a microscope though it doesn't know it, so likewise, with respect to how we are so small compared to the universe, could it be that we are being seen (by God), though we can't visibly see it? Yes!

When you're alone, away from expectations and obligations, who are you? You are a soul (mind, will, and emotions). Is it eternal? Receive Jesus Christ for an eternal soul.

When we're alone, we also realize we are mere mortals of flesh and blood, made to know the blood of Jesus that washes us as white as snow! Just believe in receive Him in faith!

International: *Eternal-tional* *All this world is meant to know King Jesus!

To give up things is to give… up (to God)

Let go is to let… go (to help yourself move forward)

Relate with the Redeemer so that we will want to experience relay "le" (to pass Him on to others)…. le (Him). "Re-late" showing it's never too late, as long as you're alive! Sometimes we have to re-lay with Him in the manger, even the best manager, to see how we were originally meant to deem, to know Him.

The "t" shaped cross ("te") is for you ("te", in Spanish).

Whoa, we came from something (a wo-man, the wo-rold)

Succumb your stance towards your circumstances towards the circumference of God agape unfailing love.

To stand under (God's omniscience) is to understand!

The world and science is based off of doubtful *if's*. The promises of God are based off of eternally guaranteed *is's*.

If we all were to stop striving to figure things out on our own, we would see them through the lens of faith, through knowing God.

Who is Jesus for? *Jeez, us! (Je-sus)*

Je-sus: Je sounds like *de*, meaning *of in* Spanish, the most commonly communicated language that uses English words (that are used in this book)

Sus means *your* in Spanish

(Of your… being!)

Biblio-techa: *Biblio* pointing to the Bible. All the answers you try to look for about life are fulfilled in the Bible.

*Think of folks saying "Pray for Israel", event in Ukraine, and birds falling from the sky for no reason (how they correlate with verses in the Bible).

Continue to use the key from the other page when reading these other Christ inspired readings, too!

Relearning Our 123's
By Samantha Wilezol

Uni-Verse
Uni (one)-God
Bi-ble
Tri-nity

Uni: one
Bi: two
Tri: three
*And the risen cross of Jesus has four sides!

Relearning our A-Z's
By Samantha Wilezol

God is the Alpha and Omega, like the first and last letter of the Greek alphabet pointing to scientific translation.

What *Seri* in online-talking map directions Teaches Us About The Bible
By Samantha Wilezol

Just like how *Seri* in online-talking map directions may take us down weird looking roads, we know it leads us to our final destination, even when we don't always understand it. The satellites are from above, so it's not for us to fully understand, but to simply trust. Likewise, even when we don't always understand the Bible, we can know it's not for us to always fully understand, but to simply trust, and how heaven is our eternal home (because God is only Omniscient, Omnipresent, and Omnipotent. Also, the Bible was given from above, like how *Seri* satellites come from above).

Signs of God's Love (Continued):
By Samantha Wilezol

The Holy Spirit (3 in One), like water and clouds can be in 3 forms, but still the same thing. He is omniscient, omnipotent, and omnipresent!

Let the Risen Cross Cross Paths With You:
By Samantha Wilezol

Jesus is needed to live! (see John verses).

God has been trying to get your attention through cross roads, cross walks, and the compass rose (shape of a risen cross), pointing to the risen cross of Jesus. We cannot escape Him, wherever we are! That is how much He loves us.

Humble Yourself to Christ
By Samantha Wilezol

Research *What was the first vision of the world?* And *First Vision* comes up. Let that speak to you.

feelings are not the truth of God's Word. They have no power over you.
Gawk sounds like *God.* Let's gawk in admirable awe at God's goodness!

The Shirt
By Samantha Wilezol

I got a new shirt, and I decided it would represent something new.
Optimism.
Freedom.
Joy.
In Christ Jesus!
*Elaboration on this in link, link listed on the page from some previous pages ago!

Signs From Above:

The wind (unseen, but can be felt) is a sign that God is real, and 3 things in one (3 forms water takes, but is still one, and 3 forms clouds take, but are still one, like the Trinity) point to Him. And Jesus is of *jeez, us!*

For Wally
By Samantha Wilezol

I used to work with a great friend named Wally, and when I would fill up the ice bucket when Wally was washing dishes, ideas would be shared of very inspiring things pointing to God that I never forgot. When I would work as a hostess, I would write what would be said on napkins so I wouldn't forget.

Said by Wally, put into words by Samantha Wilezol:

Waiting upon God isn't sitting around doing nothing just waiting. It's actually serving him.

Knowing God's truth is our protection from the enemy's lies.

"Confidence" means "with faith".

In a rocking chair, you feel like you are doing something when worrying, but don't get anywhere.

When we change the way we see things, those things change

Take the past out of the present, and you have the future.

"Amen" means "it is what it is".

It's not what you don't have, it's what you have.

You have to LET God be your power source (be fully plugged in).

The word Easter originated from something false,
so the true meaning of Resurrection Day points to the
truth of Jesus Christ!
Me seeing that God is my crutch and umbrella!

For Wally (Continued)
By Samantha Wilezol

Wally and Samantha W.!

This is the bag of napkins I have of the notes I took from what was shared!

*Note to readers: Link to pictures in this book, including cover picture, below for a bigger/ clearer view of them, including original haikus by Samantha Wilezol, too: https://docs.google. com/document/d/1uwGfeRIX40TbLk4MmYllp_wnmYllLWl5PAhRV5vuC-A/edit?usp=sharing

Writings of Samantha Wilezol for Christ continued:

HEADLIGHTS
Put on your headlights, and go in faith, knowing God is guiding your steps.

TRAFFIC LIGHT
A traffic light is like how God always says, yes, no, or wait to our prayers.

TRESURE
Looking for a verse is like looking for hidden treasure.

SEA SALT OR ROAD SALT (is your favorite the beach or wintery climates?)

Other things can't compare!
By Samantha Wilezol

We can now say "Doo doo" to doing, "poo" to trying to prove, "wishy washy" to worldy "wishing" instead of faith, and <<Sigh>>, ertttt! (siren sound) to science.

Wish vs Faith
By Samantha Wilezol

Wish is based off of chance, but faith is based off of guarantee of Jesus!

Happiness vs Joy
By Samantha Wilezol

Happiness is based off of external temporary circumstances, but joy comes from an inner eternal promise, King Jesus!

One of my favorite verses:

Luke 14:11D:
"But if you're content to be simply yourself, you will become more than yourself." (MSG version)

Hope For You
Original material by Samantha Wilezol

Calling all people of all continents of God's world, if you're a pastor, scientist, student, or someone still trying to figure it all out, there's hope for you. His name is Jesus.

Striving
Original material by Samantha Wilezol

Who are you? Are you what you do? What are you striving for? Let's rather thrive in knowing Christ. Because when you're alone, you are a mere mortal meant to know Jesus Christ.

Soldiers, Put Your Swords Down
Original material by Samantha Wilezol

I saw all soldiers of the world put their swords down, when they settled the internal spiritual battle inside of them. Because you can't have a physical war with just one person. They came to see there was no more flesh and blood to fight, but rather just an inner spiritual battle in all of us, that Jesus can settle. All we need is the sword of the Spirit for ourselves.

Readers, read Ephesians 6!

- Readers, see my colored chart with John 1:1 in Amplified Version of Laminin and years explained in link in this book (from some previous pages prior).

  If Jesus wasn't real, than the Bible couldn't be real. Jesus points to the Bible and the Bible points to Jesus. Also, the universe points to Jesus.

Friends I could wear a lie detector, while sharing my testimony, but ultimately, an eye witness account speaks for itself. Like the "I" of the Universe speaking for itself.

Note for readers: In the writings below, I felt led by the Holy Spirit to mention any life experiences that any general person might go through. God personally delivered me from spending a lot of excess time on my school studies, and can deliver you from anything!

The Cure
By Samantha Wilezol

If I thought I'd be the cure, why is there still unforgiveness in the world?

If sarcasm were the cure, why can't it take pain away?

If forming your own identity were the cure, why do you still wonder of what your identity is?

If the cure was finding our identity in what we do, we wouldn't have to say "There's more work that still has to be done."

If marriage were the cure, why is there still loneliness or striving, if it's not done the holy way?*

If I were the cure, I wonder why I can't change the world, make everyone happy, or save the world from death.

If I could save myself, there wouldn't be a need for saving.

If people were the cure, I don't have to wonder why something greater would have to come.

If research on human intellect were the cure, I wonder why some people spend their whole lives trying to find answers and never find them.

If a vacation were the cure, I wonder why where ever you go, there you are.

If more fame were the cure, I wonder why I feel unnoticed inside.

If more make up were the cure, I wonder why I still feel ugly on the inside.

If attempting to look more strong on the outside were the cure, I wonder why it is stemmed from feeling weak on the inside, or having been told so when younger.

If sports were the cure, I wonder why my team doesn't always win.

If more doing or more rules in religion were the cure, I wonder why some still feel unbelief.

If more sex were the cure, I wonder why some still feel unloved on the inside.

If minding your own business and living and let live were the cure, I wonder why sin still finds people out.

If my cookie cutter, big house were the cure, I wonder why I still feel cut up and small on the inside.

If my conscience were the cure, I wonder why it can be lost.

If the big bang in science were the cure I wonder why there's still "if" .

If medication were the cure, I wonder why just Jesus was able to heal me.

So what could be the cure?

Could it be God's love? Absolutely.

Since God's love is the cure, I can put the negative talk down.

Since God's love is the cure, I can put the make up brush down.

Since God's love is the cure, soldiers can put their weapons down.

Since God's love is the cure, I can live with myself now.

And see myself and the world for how God intended it.

To know Him and share His love with others until He calls me home.

*God's way!

Jesus is the cure.

The Intercession
Original material by Samantha Wilezol

When I didn't have enough money to eat, or was too afraid to eat, something still fed me.

When I was too sick to get sunlight from outside, something still gave me light.

When I was too sick, to be able to breathe on my own, something breathed into me.

When water in my land was too dirty to drink or I didn't have enough money to pay the water bill, something still quenched my thirst.

Who was it?

Jesus Christ, the bread, breath, light and living water of the world.

*Readers, see verses in John in Bible!

Behind the Mask
Original material by Samantha Wilezol

My laughing used to be stemmed from inner pain.

My smiling used to be stemmed from inner brokenness.

My strive towards much make up, was stemmed from feeling made up on the inside.

But I learned to take off the mask, to see freedom in Christ.

The More I Believe, The More I See
Original material by Samantha Wilezol

The more I believe, the more I see I don't want the drink anymore.

The more I believe, the more I see I don't need the worldly fame anymore.

The more I believe, the more I see the One who can change me through the renewing of my mind.

The more I believe, the more I see those past things don't own me anymore, but rather who calls me His.

Jesus Christ.

*(B comes before C in the alphabet, and B before C in B.C. in Before Christ; B (first) believe to C see)

Like a Princess
Original material by Samantha Wilezol

I see I can live out the fruits of the spirit, like the character of a princess, but investing eternally, not internally.

*elaboration in link from some pages prior.

The One Only Original Founding Father
Original material by Samantha Wilezol

The One that made our states united in the beginning is the one that can bring us back to that. Conduct was more orderly when the scriptures of Jesus were studied amongst kids. It points to King Jesus!

Wish vs Hope
By Samantha Wilezol

You see wish is a chanceful "hope", but faith is a guaranteed hope in Christ Jesus.

Being "lucky" is based off of chance, but being blessed is
based off of undeserved favor. From Christ.

*Note for readers: In the writing below, I felt led by the Holy Spirit to mention any life experiences that any general person might go through. God personally delivered me from spending a lot of excess time on my school studies, and can deliver you from anything!

If I Was Enough
By Samantha Wilezol

If I was enough, I wonder why my good looks or good
efforts couldn't have avoided the divorce.

If I was enough, I wonder why my good parenting couldn't
have avoided my kid from crying a lot.

If I was enough, I wonder why I now feel like I'm running
out of love in myself to give to my spouse.

If I was enough, I wonder why my life-long good eating and
vitamins couldn't have avoided me death.

If my house was enough, I wonder why it couldn't have
avoided me from feeling unsafe at times.

If a vacation was enough, I wonder why where you go, there you are.

If I was enough, I wonder why my church attendance being encouraged
on my kid couldn't have avoided them turning into a prodigal.

If I was enough, I wonder why the number of good deeds I did and number of religious
rules I kept couldn't have answered the question of "Am I good enough for heaven?"

If I was enough, I wonder why I couldn't have changed that person's heart.

If humans, or worldly love, or inclusive University education, or laws, or corporations,
or systems, or politics were enough, I wonder why there's still war.
Mistrust.
Division.

So what is enough? How about the One who is enough, so I
don't have to strive to be. Who can change any heart.

His Name is Jesus.

If We Had It All Together
By Samantha Wilezol

If you and I had it all together, why is it hard to explain or to grasp our emotions sometimes? Or why do we cry, or have trantrums sometimes, or feel inner desperation? Or why does the greatest CEO of a company who is spending his whole life trying to prove something, do it out remembering being told he was nothing when he was five years old?

Why Worldly Marriages Don't Last
By Samantha Wilezol

Worldly marriages that are not done in Jesus's way don't last because they're under obligation, under a law. Love with Jesus is under pure love, not a law. Why? Because Jesus came to abolish the law, and the law is now love. *Readers, see verse of Jesus pointing to that!

From Striving To Thriving
By Samantha Wilezol

We are all striving or reaching. For some, for something. We all have expectations, obligations, motivations, or impulses we live by every day. Do you ever look at many cars passing by and wonder where they are going or what are they chasing after? Life is like traffic light signals and turn and slow down and speed up signs, but what is right? Does it feel like sometimes you can't find what you're chasing after or sometimes you forget what you're chasing after? Or wonder why you are doing so? Do you ever doubt yourself? This route of life can seem like street signs a lot of slow down speed ups or turn this way, but what way is right? No matter what we're striving for, we all can't escape disappointment, time marching on, our bodies getting older (how we are not constant), and the question of did I reach what I was striving for? Some may feel like they're on a hamster wheel, how you get up, you work, have some time for yourself, you go to bed, and repeat, and you may wonder how can I get out of this circle? Or maybe you've been through so much and you feel like you can't sit alone with your thoughts, so you go out and drink to try and numb the pain, but then the temporary numbness wears off, so you feel like you have to go back to the drink. Maybe you feel like you're on a hamster wheel with that and you don't know how to get out of it. Or maybe you're someone who's been through so much and feel you've been hurt by people, so you I want to spend time alone and you may wonder, When will I be freed of this emotional rut?

Also, even at night, your head may hit the pillow and you said you're tired.

You may get the title of what you do in life for your job and you know it in your head, but does it ever satisfy your heart? Just because you get a lot of attention at your job, do you ever still feel un noticed? Or unloved ? Does it ever feel like there's just something missing on the deep down inside of you, that no matter if your mind thinks you "have it all" or that things are going good, something still feels missing? Or, just because you're around people throughout the day, do you ever still feel lonely? Do you ever wonder what you're doing "all of this" for? Perhaps there's a phase of your mind that thinks you "have it all together" but then the next it resorts to thinking the opposite, of "what am I trying to prove"? You may think, and this thought will come to you at some point in your life, "what I am doing all this striving for"? You see, because there's a contrast. The more humans try to elevate themselves in position, status, etc. in their own human strength, they feel empty and striving on the inside because there is a contrast. Do you ever feel like that? What could be this contrast, what is this light that shines brighter than the dark in us?

Jesus. Apart from Jesus, we are nothing on the inside. The Bible says we were made from the dust, intended in the very beginning to know Him and worship him.

When you're alone, who are you? When you lay down for the night, your makeup off or your tie off, look up at the ceiling for a minute before drifting off to sleep, or you look at yourself in the mirror, expectations put to the side. who are YOU? Not what you DO? If no one were to tell you who you are, if that title or accomplishment now ran thin on you that once tried to tell you who you are, who are YOU?

When you run out of energy to tell yourself positive affirmations, who are you?

Are you able to say with confidence everything is going to be OK just because it may be said you are a lawyer, or teacher, have a doctorate, a decent conscious, a home owner, etc. Does the source in which you are trying to get your hope or identity sustain you inwardly? Or do you feel like you need more and more and don't know where that "more" ends to satisfy that void on the inside? Do you ever feel like sometimes you can't find what you're trying to chase after? And that this striving is maybe making you feel empty on the deep down inside? Just because you were a teacher or a homeowner, does everything end up being OK? Even when you tell yourself positive affirmations, do you view that everything end up being OK? Could your phd have avoided that sickness, your conscious to have avoided that decision that changed your life in a weird way? So what is the set in stone truth that everything will be ok, not phrases said to "just merely make me feel better"?

We all have many expectations on ourselves and from others, so if they fluctuate or we don't meet them, does our value or identity change as a person? If our family members or friends left us or don't support what we do anymore, does my value change? And even if we answer no that sometimes, why do some people still choose to give up or doubt themselves? Why can't we escape death even? As time progresses, some people don't recognize themselves anymore or want to start over or go back to day 1 of their lives.

What if I told you there is a love that can meet you where you're at and his name is Jesus Who can give you a new name and fresh start? Hence the name Jesus meaning, " he of you", and that you can revisit the Redeemer to discover what you were really deemed, or made for. It's in Him. Also, we can learn more about him through the Bible, which the words "vive el" are pronounced as Bible, meaning Live He (Jesus). El means el in Spanish *the* and *he* spelling the same thing.

We may think we have it all together or that our conscience is strong, but then something may happen in life that happens in a way we thought it wouldn't, so it may change the way you think or the way you live or adapt to everyday life or how you carry yourself. Sometimes, even if we think our conscience or good intentions in the beginning were good, we may become a person we said we were never going to become. Or perhaps you may become afraid of the future and you wonder why your conscious may left or why all your good effort couldn't have changed that person or stopped that that thing to not happen. From that, it may be hard for you to trust in yourself or on other people, so you may go to a drink or social media which may give you temporary false hope or numbness, but then your mind goes back to realizing that that problem is still there, an unsolved one. So what can solve it?

Could it be this Jesus, who is of you, hence the name "Je-sus"?
Yes. Ya way, not no way (Yah-Way is a name of God).
You can have all the love and money in the world, but still may be sick or
sad. So you start looking for a source of hope that can satisfy.
Let Jesus be your hope, friends!

Part Two:

Lets say you're driving in your car one day and a random person comes up to you and says "I love you, and here is a $100 Starbucks gift card for you." How would you react? You don't even know them and didn't do anything for them. But they say that they know you.

A retired individual from the Coastguard got my suitcase in 7 lanes of traffic when I was little. My Grandpa, Ron, wouldn't stop loving on me, though I wasn't fully receptive & not fully open to him yet. That's like King Jesus! Who is God? God is love.

We can rest in knowing that Jesus is true and we don't have to strive anymore, we can rest in Him. Like the wind, the more we experience it, we don't have to doubt it at all. It's all faith in Jesus.

The amount of good deeds or rituals I do in other religions can't answer the question of "Did I do enough for heaven?" Also, if I waited to answer if I needed Jesus because I thought I had more time, why do time run out on some? We are finite. Only God is infinite.

He is the constance we are looking for. When we're alone in our beds at night, we realize we are a living being that is getting older day by day, so we are finite.

And so my friends, I think we see that as humans we are very complex creatures. But some words speak for themselves in that Jesus is 'of us', so will you let yourself be of him and live for him? He is the promised peace for all and the world.

Receive Jesus today. John 3:16, Romans 10:9, consider the cost
extra thought for the readers:
Apart from Jesus, we are nothing on the inside. The Bible says we were made from the dust, intended in the very beginning to know Him and worship him.

Santa Can Retire
By Samantha Wilezol
Why would we want to believe in anything else like Santa when we know God satisfies so much better, satisfies your soul, works outside of time, so you never outgrow Him? God can meet your reality and show you eternity.

Who Are You When You're Alone?
By Samantha Wilezol

So when you look up at the ceiling before falling asleep, your make up or tie off from the day, who are you? We're all just mere flesh bone and blood mortals who are made from the dust, less than what *we* were striving for from the day, originally made in the image of God, in need of a Savior made to glorify God, through receiving Jesus. So we don't have to strive anymore; we can rest in Jesus. We can find rest for our souls. Readers, read verse about from the dust.

Readers: refer to the same key from some prior pages ago of "Shapes, Words, etc." that can help you to think about what section each of these Christ-inspired original concepts fit into!

Further Original Biblical Points, that can also relate to an artist's view:
By Samantha Wilezol

We remember we were made in God's image, it's just we don't remember. Sin is the amnesia that separated us.

Bless is to "b less".

When we may feel Insecure.. we are actually in secure in Him! Our emotions do not define the Truth of God.

We are won by One and one of One!

Ministry ..." winistry" : Jesus has won for us!

He sees you because he sees you, because he sees you, because he sees you. He loves you because he loves you, because he loves you. He knows you because he knows you because he knows you. He wants you because he wants you, because he wants you. The most pure love in the universe.

What love made the love that made the love that made the love that made the love to make you, to know you? The Maker, King Jesus!

****Note to readers this section is to remind us, in faith that the Bible is indeed true:*******

Friendly note to readers: All these typed works in this whole book are originals by Samantha Wilezol, even if my name is not next to every single line / paragraph. Ultimately, all glory to Jesus for the opportunity to share!

To be it (el bi b le) Bible, and el Bible (bee-blay) points to El Vive (of Jesus), who points to all of life (We are who He is, just receive Him in faith)

Bible: You to become it so you could become he, to see the way you were meant to be. And when you look in the mirror " le" sees "el" in mirror. He sees you when you see him so you don't have to strive to be anything else so that you don't have to not recognize yourself anymore

We couldn't know before we knew we were known, so the supernatural is simply to trust

If we're not under the old testament anymore, why is the Old Testament still in the Bible?*****

We were like fish, who swam in schools, the rules of the Old Testament, so we eventually could dive into the depths of his grace.

We graduated from the old rules to enter into the new, who knew, to see the good news.

we are not under the rules of the old covenant anymore so we can graduate into Grace, the new, who knew!

It's to become you, he became you so you could see him, in the model He left of life, el vive, so you will want to become like him.

No scientist knows the number of grains of sand on the seashore, but they represent thoughts. So it's known by someone.

Further proof the Bible is real, Our ultimate confidence being faith
(continued:)****

- "Bebe" means to drink the living water, which sounds like Bible
- It's like God is the autotroph of life. We are just the heterotrophs of the four things that he is.
- If minding your own business were the cure, then the "I am" wouldn't be in the business of seeing your business.
- B comes before C- alphabet and time points to (BC)- We need to believe first to see.
- When we stand under, we'll see things for how they are helping us to understand through a lens of faith.
- When I see Grace (c), I'll see beyond the grave
- Even storms have an eye
- The four things: proof he is of you, and that what we are is who he is. Just received and believe him in faith, confess your sins to him. That is proof we don't have to strive towards becoming what we want to be. Just to be, to be alive, is to believe him before we leave to heaven with him!
- Mind you, but you know have a new mind in Him
- God is love and he just wants to relate with you

- Extra things: why doesn't God still verbally speak today and big miracles still happened today?
- Answer: He ascended! To believe is to be alive to leave. We hear him now in our hearts so it's strengthening our faith.
- Question, why does God still allow hunger and war?
- Answer: Well, succumb your stance towards your circumstances to the circumference of God's ending love.

History View:

- There's artifact evidence of Jesus in the Bible, but we don't doubt history books, though the person and artifacts aren't sitting on our desks. We have to experience it! Going to space and building the first airplane sounded different, but it happened. Miracles in the Bible may sound "out of the ordinary", but let it happen to you.

- When you're in the eye of a storm, you may not realize you're in the eye and see the storm, so you may say *there's a storm!* Are you in it or of it? If you're "I" centered you may say you're in it, but if you're God centered ("o", like the perfect orbit shape of the planets), you'll see the storm doesn't have to get in you, relating to Peter walking on the water towards Jesus.
- Bullet point below applicable to any generic situation that anyone may go through:
- Some may wonder why their learning please and thank you, and being told where to go couldn't have prevented them from turning into another person they thought they wouldn't become.
- Jesus is greater than trials!
- * see my next writing snippet about how we were divided by sin, but then Jesus came.*

Once again, we may wonder why doesn't God still perform big miracles, stop world hunger, or speak verbally today; It is to strengthen our faith and because He is ascended and speaks to our heart. Succumb your stance towards your circumstances to the circumference of God's unfailing love towards you, His circle. Seeing chameleons changing colors and their eyes in different directions is like seeing the miracle of the donkey talking in the Bible, in addition to seeing parrots talking today! Also, being in the eye of a storm is like when God parted the Red Sea for Moses to walk through on dry land!

Holey (cheese)
Holy: (Jesus came for jeez, us, because we were holey)
Wholey (keys to heaven)
The holy came to fix what was holey, so we could be made whole through, becoming holy too

1D: one way we were intended to deem
2D: Bi- ble (today receive him)
3D: Tri-nity (on the third day he was raised)
4D: four directions in the world, four corners of Cross
Read the Bible to experience it in 3-D to experience God in 4D in heaven!

Succumb your stand towards your circumstances, towards the circumference of God's agape unfailing love towards you.

Faith is trusting to become entrusted to be known and shown the unknown, to see the secret of the universe, and be given the key of heaven.

Let his embrace brace you to face life.

More Biblical Thoughts
By Samantha Wilezol

Old testament to New Testament: Monarch butterflies still have their caterpillar form in the middle of them so they don't forget who they are. We need to read the Old Testament truth so that when we come into the New testament of his freedom, we don't get too emotion led in our freedom, so we remember where we came from, that we couldn't keep the 10 Commandments on our own because we are flawed. Have a healthy balance of truth and spirit.

Once again, a. caterpillar doesn't forget what he came from. The form of the caterpillar in the middle is still there, but it just grows wings. It's like the caterpillar form grounds him so he doesn't fly too freely without making sense of it. The Bible never contradicts itself. It may just contradict the way we think or the way we live. The miracles in the Bible point to you are the miracle in Christ. The part of the Bible you don't understand points to how God understands you. The passages that explain Jesus point to how he can relate with you in life and make you sinless.

If Jesus wasn't true, then the Bible couldn't be true. If 2+2 wasn't four, then four couldn't be 2+2.

Have you red the red? It is telling you you are loved by Jesus (the red text in the Bible).

Text from the text(book): God is telling you you are loved by Him!

Another interesting thought: Some people say they "may not have time in their day" to read the Bible, but remember, we all get 24 hours in a day, so we all make time for what is important to us! Read at least three verses a day, keep your Bible next to your bed. Also, some people listen to the Bible through an audiobook, but once again, we all get 24 hours in a day! Perhaps spend less time on social media.

*** readers, check out my other writings and talks!

Second writing and talk:
(The Bible more broken down and what faith really is. Take his word for it. He is the source, he is reliable, we could not know during the unknown, so how could we know? Faith is trusting to become entrusted to be shown the unknown to see the secret of the universe, and be given the key of heaven.)

Third talk and writing:
(Further explanation about how we were separated from God)

Fourth talk:
(What Jesus really wants to be in our lives. Relate drawings, and if Christianity was about doing, Jesus would not have had bad encounters with religious people.)

5th talk
(What it means to live the holy life for God.)
The more I study, the more I know what the answer is in a test before I see the other answer choices. I won't be tempted by the world's ways. The world is trying to tell you your worth through a number on a dollar, but when we take off the number, it's just paper. Keep your eye out for the bait It's trying to give you. Words as the words in the word tell you who you are, which defines your worth in the Bible in Christ.

Also, a change in root yields a change in fruit, see what he wants to be and do in your life. Grace is the good race!

Endeavoring into more Christ centered thoughts:
by Samantha Wilezol

Cool Side Thoughts:
- Our faith can help us to walk on water like Peter, and jet skiing and wake boarding is a cool analogy to see that!
- Cold stars are red and hot stars are blue
- Even though a driveway should be called a parkway and a parkway should be called a driveway, we adapt to it

Ions and a Flashlight Battery Analogy
By Samantha Wilezol

We have positive and negative ions in our body like the positive and negative sides of a battery in a flashlight. When we line up the opposite of what we think to be true (the positive side next to the other side), or when we line up the opposite with what is, we'll see a solution that it actually works. In Mr. D AMoore's class from high school, I worked with the ions. It's like God is the I of the ions. When we are willing to experience the opposite of what we think or skeptize, we then see that it works. If you were to skepticsize, "how could the positive side of the battery work when it's lined up to the opposite?" it wouldn't be proven until you actually experience it. When we are willing to experience the Word, we can then take it's Word for it. So what is truth? It is what works. Could it be there is something (one) thing that works for everyone when we let ourselves experience it? God!

Side note: (Even if the instructions look weird, like instructions in a different language before putting a stool together or directions on a ride before riding it on the boardwalk, we can trust it.

****More original analogies by Samantha Wilezol, that help us to understand that it is indeed, true, that Jesus had to become mere like us, so that we could find strength in him when we surrender of ourselves. Also, when we experience things opposite to the way we think in our human minds, like experiencing God, our initial doubt that we thought we had before is drowned out, in his love:

We have about 75% of water in our bodies and brains, so this analogy is applicable to anyone.

For water to be purified, like in water bottles, reverse osmosis is done, which is molecules going from an area of concentration that is high to the opposite. Relate that to how the ultimate strength (God) become humble so that the humble (us)could become strong in him.

We view warm as hot and cold as blue, but red stars are cold and cold stars are hot. God may know things we don't know.

The opposite side of a magnet attracts the other; you may feel yourself being attracted to God right now- just let it happen, like how the polls of the earth work.

There are sound waves underwater. There is much more of the ocean to be explored. God knows things that we don't know.

Our parasympathetic system works for us of the opposite of what we're thinking. (When we're in a fight or flight mode).

Drink the Bebe of his vive. El vive, the higher power, the lasting real high.

His light is actually light, not a burden, like how our eyes (pupils) open up more when we see light.

If we don't need the rules anymore, why is the Old Testament still there? A ruler (the Old Testament rules) helps us to see the measure (of freedom in Christ) we've been given (so we know how to work the measure) (VER in Universe).

The Viewmaster Analogy
By Samantha Wilezol

When you want to know what a word means, you go to the root of it (el Bible, also le Bible, means "Him to be you" and also "you to be Him" when you break down the syllables). Also, "Jesus" sounds like "Jeez, us!" and Je-sus of Jesus and -*heh! yours*! (Pronounce *heh* as enthusiastic)

The device of a Viewmaster may look old and boring, but when you experience it, it proves to be the opposite! They take paper discs to see the full picture.

Likewise, skeptics may look at the paper pages of the Bible before experiencing it, and think that it looks old and outdated, but when you experience the Bible, your initial once doubt is drowned out in His love.

Also, when you shine light on a negative (*negative* the term used for the form of a photo before it is developed), it shows a positive (form of a photo), similar to our lives, and a master, like in the word view master is a "he" like "se" in Universe. God!

Let your correct view of the Viewmaster change your view of the Master, that he just wants to shine some light on you to show you the full picture of what you were meant to be in Him!

The ideas keep on flowing from the Holy Spirit!
By Samantha Wilezol

Note to readers: once again, as you read, think about what category each of these paragraphs can fit in, like educational views helping us to understand God more, or relating it to miraculous animals that God has made, etc.)

See below:

"Jeez, us!" sounds like Jesus, and Jesus is of "Je-sus" (-heh! yours!) Pronounce heh as enthusiastic)

If Christianity was about rules, then Jesus would not have had bad experiences with religious people. If Jesus wasn't good, then he wouldn't be of us. If it was about doing, we would've have had to do something before becoming a human who needs the four elements to live, who Jesus is in Himself (see John verses).

Fireflies are a miracle from God and talking parrots, similar to the talking donkey in the Bible!

When we let ourselves experience God, we can then take the Word's (the Bible's) word for it!

Research shows a synonym of the Bible is the "Good Book". It is good indeed!

The good news sounds like the good knews!

Lattice in math is a cool analogy to show how God sees much further than we can see ourselves!

An analogy referring to a stage we all experienced when we were born:

What was the first novel that relates to your naval, the cord when you were in your mother's womb that was giving you the four things that you need that points to who those four things is (see John verses(, who gives your eternal label of who you are in Him.

We say "aaa" (yawn) when we wake up in the morning and say "zzz" (zzzz's) when we sleep. We are unconsciously making room for the unknown, who is the Alpha and Omega, beginning and the end. Also, 12am and 12pm is like how God has no beginning and end!

Stop trying to find out *tu vive* so that El vive (pronounced as bee-blay) can find you, of el Bible (bee-blay). (Le vive, His life, who "laid" in a manger). Who, el, is for Jeez, us! Jesus.

Stop trying to figure out life Athrough Z. Wait, what? Yeah! It sounds familiar because it is, the soundness of sounds!

Stop trying to figure out life so that the Ultimate Figure (God) can find you. Some people say how math and science helps us to learn more about life, so let's let it help us learn more about life through an eternal lens.

(The figure): 1*1 we are of (*) One, which yields one. When we receive him, we are One Spirit with him.

A ruler helps us to see the measure of faith (and His grace and love) we've been given, so we don't misinterpret it; The infinite measure, so we don't need to be under the (rules) anymore of the Old Testament.

Why can we hear underwater but not in space? Because we need to stand under to understand (what is being said to us from above, from *outer*, which is not of us, but is meant to be for us).

(After all, we were like organisms who swam when we were in our mother's womb, made in, His image, and His living water).

Papel- "Pap el".. "Dad He".. all of paper and books points to Jesus how Jesus is the ultimate answer!

All of direction (SEWN) points to how we were sewn by God in our mothers womb.

The breath that gave us a second breath that is proven to be of us is of Jeez us, pointing to how it's Jesus, and the force went straight to our heart showing that it's love. Thank you Jesus.

Another big question:

When the veil was torn into, is that when the big landmass on earth divided into seven continents? Like how seven in the seven continents represent fullness?

Just like how some people see colors when they play music, reading the Bible is like putting on glasses that helps us to see color when we are colorblind without him. When we hear a verse, it reminds us of how we were meant to be. Like when someone hears a verse in an older song in a nursing home, it helps them to remember.

If you wear a shirt that says "Le", when you look in the mirror, it will read "el". When we look in the mirror, we see Him so that we will see we were intended to be like him.

Light travels quicker than sound and light years in OUTER space. We need to trust the light, Jesus, that helps us to then understand.

Let God "fax" the facts to your heart.

If this world was about doing, then, the risen cross wouldn't be hugging you to relate to you with a heart around it

The risen cross of Jesus has been trying to get your attention through crossword puzzles, and similar to a wordsearch, the Word searches for us. The answer key is the keys to Heaven through Jesus!

The four corners of the earth forever point to Christ!

I heard a lady at the library said, "Why did I put myself through college just for a degree?" The degree can change what you do, but it doesn't change who you are as a person. Your title doesn't change who you are as a person

Hidden treasures revealed in Christ!

Put on your headlights and go in faith!

His embrace braces us to face life!

You caught a shooting star, a starfish, something of above and of God's ocean!

An original analogy to reach out to teens using teen terminology to reach them:

"You're so cool", the sun didn't move any further away, so you wouldn't burn up. "You're so hot", the sun didn't move any closer to so you wouldn't freeze up. God controls the orbit of the planets!

Reading the old testament: It's like boosters on a rocket in that when we reach the higher altitude of knowing Christ, the boosters of the Old Testament fall off because we are not under the rules anymore of the Old Testament.

I'm not here to get merely "preachy", but to share God's living truth with you that is more than mere words!

Colossians 2:17 is the verse that talks about a shadow of what is to come.

Humans have became kings in history many times, but only Jesus, the One true King, became a baby to then save the world of their sins!

Lucky vs blessed

You caught a shooting star:
By Samantha Wilezol

You caught a shooting star, a starfish, which is proof of how the supernatural met with the natural (us), the stars in the sky and of the universe before we were born to know, pointing to the star of Bethlehem and the Greek word for fish, pointing to Jesus, showing that you were with God when He spoke things into existence and made in His image when He formed you in your mother's room (we were like fish, when we were essentially living in water in our mother's womb).

Also, if you stand with your arms and legs out, you're in the same shape as a starfish!

Also, you were on his mind when he performed the miracles and died on the cross for your sins and rose from the grave three days later.

So we don't have to "wish upon a star" anymore, since we've already caught one and been shown One, ultimately Jesus! ** sidenote, when I was little, there was a starfish on my uncle's roof. I don't know how it got there, but I believe in faith it was a sign of God!

We are one in the One who has won!

Time Was Counting Down to When He Would Come
so time is now counting up to when He will return!
By Samantha Wilezol

Similar to when time was counting down, predestining when Jesus was born, time counted down. What was predestined to come has arrived! We currently count down to await something new entering into a new year, before a rocket takes off, and before food is ready in the microwave. Open the door to indulge in the Lord, like opening the door of a microwave! The Bible talks of how He stands at the door and knocks.

He is ready and waiting for you. Decide you want to be ready for God because He's ready for you. None of us know when our last day is going to be, so use the time you have been given.

People can't tangibly explain what love looks like. There's acts of love, but what does love actually look like? Jesus! There's some news that sounds too good to be true, and the good news is holy, so it is true!

The Word Universe And Time Counting Backwards
By Samantha Wilezol

~ ~~ Who decided to call the word "universe" the "universe"? Of course God did, who gave the revelation to the first person. He named it based off of what he saw because he decided that time should count backwards, awaiting the One that he saw. The individual who decided time to count backwards was a monk, which can relate to Christian monasticism, research shows, proof that the supernatural wants to meet your natural, no matter how you were once raised or what you want believed, because apparently he works outside of time.

Growth on earth even points to God, how flowers grow in a circle position. Research the first vision.

Vive el - the life - Bible

"Bubble" sounds like Bible, that even though we can't see God, He is still there!

Further points from an artistic approach:
By Samantha Wilezol
See next page below

Jesus Was Our Landline:
By Samantha Wilezol

It's like we were fish who were swimming in our mother's womb. When we were delivered into the real world, it's like our naval, that was feeding a source, was the button going off, saying, "We need a landline, we need a landline!"; because we were delivered into land (born into the world), no longer swimming in "God's living water", originally made in His image. It's like Jesus was our landline that saved us at right the right time, giving us the four things we need to survive that who he is (air, water, food, and sunlight), even apart from the cord (umbilical cord), we were once attached to.

We Are Unknowingly Making Room For The Unconscious
By Samantha Wilezol

It's like we make ourselves known to the unknown when we make room for the unconscious, when we fall asleep to refresh our conscience for the next day. We give up control each day, whether or not we realize it in the dark, and when we're alone; in which some people are afraid of the dark or of being alone, so why are we afraid to give up to God in the light?

You Were There
By Samantha Wilezol

It's like you were there when God spoke the Earth into existence, and when He rose from the grave three days later, and when He performed the miracles in the Bible that He still does. You were in His mind. We were unknown during the unknown, so we couldn't know before we were known. We existed when we were essentially swimming creations in our mother's womb; just because we don't remember doesn't mean it didn't happen. Mind you, but you get a new mind in Christ, so he reminds you of what you can't remember yourself.

God Has Been Revealing Himself To You
By Samantha Wilezol

God has been revealing himself to you. You just haven't let yourself realize it yet. That the wind represents God that can be experienced though it can't be seen; That water that takes three forms, but is the same thing can point to the Trinity. And that the four things that you need to survive are the four things that he is. Just let yourself realize it now to believe it.

Text From The Text

When you turn on your phone, you see an Apple icon in the beginning, like how an apple was there in the beginning (Genesis).

An iceberg diagram in psychology can teach us about God (see below)

Could it be that the unconscious was affecting our conscious before we could even know it? Like how in psychology, the "Id" within the unconscious, or the unknown, creates our identity (God within the heavenly realms, creates our identity). And like the supernatural that is greater than our super ego can humble our ego.

There's something so much greater under than only what we can see about ourselves. God!

75% of our brains water have water. Be purified in His water!
Our pupils dilating to see more of His light! See His light!

Stand under to understand - By Samantha Wilezol

Another Umbilical Cord Approach
By Samantha Wilezol

Before you were brought into this world, you were attached to an umbilical cord that gave you the four things that you need. When you entered into this world, that cord was cut off from you; you were sin, or without it, the Source of all life. So the only thing that is perfect and constant had to come to become those four things for you. To save your life. As babies, we all cried and whined, and now we may think being "perfect is not crying or whining", but I think we all did that when we were younger, so we were all born in sin. Just because we don't remember, doesn't mean it didn't happen. He did it for jeez, us! Wait once again, that sounds like Someone. And He came for He to be you so that you could be him. Wait, that sounds like the name of a book broken down.

We couldn't know during the unknown, so we just have to trust to become entrusted to be shown the unknown who made himself known, so who is now known, to be shown the secrets of the universe, and be given the keys to heaven!

I'm not here to get preachy; I'm just sharing with you the natural that is of wait, the supernatural, who already experienced the natural who wants to meet your natural. Because life can be hard sometimes. But there is one who is sovereign and experienced it

Relating with someone does not need validity.

More Original deep questions, and original deep answers by Samantha Wilezol:

Where did people go after they passed before Jesus came?

I think they turned into angels because Genesis doesn't talk about how God made angels, and there was a never a year zero.

When Jesus rose again, and the veil torn in two, is that when the once one big mass land turned into seven continents?

Perhaps, because Jesus flooded the earth after Moses built the ark.

The fact that Abraham and Moses lived to be in the 100's of years in age points to how they were angels in human form, I believe in faith. I think they were getting younger in age because there was no year zero.

I think Jesus didn't just die on the cross and rise again right away, because he knew that he had to send angels to earth to minister to people who were struggling in sin.

I think he also didn't die on the cross first and rise again right away, because he wanted us to experience the contrast between our sin and him. Because, even though people had had knowledge of him in the Bible, they were still living in their sin. God wanted to send a mediator to show us the contrast between him and our sin.

I believe in faith I'm an angel, because I feel the mind of the spirit overpowering how I could think for myself. I feel like I can't think for myself, that it's only God thinking for me- (Thinking like an angel). I also remember before I was born, I remember being like a little spark floating overhead, and had dreams of flying in the sky and in general, and I even remember that happening in the sky and in space. Also, I actually remember being in the form of what is similar to an embryo in my mother's room. College taught me how to not think so He can think for me.

I'm able to recognize other angels like my brother in Christ Wally and Jim M. Jim's face looks like Jesus! The first street in Ocean City, N.J, where I like to jog is called "Jim's Place". I think Jim is James, the brother of Jesus in person. Maybe even Jesus himself, whoa. Did Jesus already return? Is it like I am dreaming right now or in heaven already, like how Ocean City is similar to heaven? Whoa!

Trust To Become Entrusted
By Samantha Wilezol

We couldn't know during the unknown, so we just have to trust to become entrusted to be shown the unknown who made himself known, so who is now known to us, to be shown the secrets of His universe, and be given the keys to heaven!

Lint….lent

"What" To "That"
By Samantha Wilezol

When we replace all of our questions about life through viewing life through the lens of the risen cross of Jesus, He shows us the answers. It is "what" to "that", "When" to "then", and "where" to "there"! The letter "W" looks like a person with both arms out, shrugging their shoulders, hence "W" sounding like "double you". Then, a lowercase "t" looks like the risen cross Jesus Christ!

Some examples are "wall" to "tall" and "will?…" to "til"! Jesus breaks down our walls with his love!

Just like how some words sound alike, like "tape for the tape", someone may think if you need scotch tape for a VHS tape, or VHS tape for scotch tape; as Christ followers, we can further explain our faith to skeptics, because skeptics can't fully understand it if it's not properly explained (if it's mistaught).

Some skeptics may argue that "C" in BC stands for "common", but ultimately, Jesus came to become the common to relate with us!

Will?… to I *will* follow Jesus!

Loving our enemies and rejoicing in trials is a way how the world will see there's something different about us for Jesus.

Is Santa a guaranteed hope? I don't think so.
By Samantha Wilezol

The average middle schooler forces their brains to think how they can weekly please other people in four different ways, in English, Science, Math, and Reading. What way is perfect? If we are not intentional about forming our own morals, than the world may choose it for us. It's no surprise that the world is corrupted since it is not believing in God. For people who gullibly buy into the world's way of thinking hurts their view of God when they get older; This can relate to the world's way of perceiving Santa, regarding Santa around Christmas; This what was thought of as innocent nurturing snowballing into the first nature of adults. If the child doesn't feel like they are measuring up to this false expectation of "perfection", then they may stop trying their best.

What causes corruption of thought of the ways of the world? Well, the Bible explains how the worries of this life,, the deceitfulness of wealth, and the desires for other things come in and choke the Word, making unfruitful. I asked my friend who is a psychologist, Beth, how often kids think about their performance or grades, and she said "weekly".

The world tries to ask kids if Santa got them everything they wanted on their wish list. Later in life, it may sadly seem odd to an adult to praise God for Himself, not just for his blessings. So let's encourage our kids to resort from stirring up greed in themselves through making Santa lists, and rather to praise God that he knows all of our needs. We must avoid the way of thinking of "Is God answering everything on my needs list?", like, "Is Santa giving me everything on my wish list?" The word "wish" connotates a "chanceful hope", but the word "faith" connotates a guaranteed hope. Is Santa a guaranteed hope? I don't think

so.

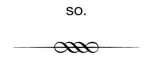

Angels point to the "angles" of people time on earth (a reflection, like how "el" reflected is "le").

Even though a telescope can't speak for itself, it "speaks" for what can be seen through it. Likewise, the Bible speaks for itself through what we can see through it.

Original Proposals by Samantha Wilezol

(These are protected on a legal level, and these within this book in general respectfully cannot be duplicated verbally or in writing- thank you for understanding. These were already spoken on on City Council levels and in Washington D.C)

Pause on the Clause
By Samantha Wilezol (see below):

Let's put a pause on the clause. This way we're teaching our kids to believe of "Have I been naughty or nice this year?" is prohibiting them from thinking that they can be under the grace of something that's for us *jeez us!* Wait, that sounds like Jesus. The way they're thinking of "Have I earned approval from my teachers or parents this year?" can influence them to think "Have I earned my way to the gifts from Santa?" So, let's put a pause on the clause and advocate for the cause of who is of us, Jesus, the roots that Ocean City and the Ocean City City Hall were rightly based off of.

The believe in Santa at a young age could prohibit adults from wanting to believe in the one true God, because they find out as adults that this once called Santa was fake. So I'd like to advocate as a professional in the Social Sciences advocating for change, for parents to have their kids in today's generation not believe in this false way of thinking; But to encourage them to believe in the one true God, who is real, who never disappoints, and who already knows all of our needs and meets them.

You see because I don't need no presents. I just need His presence; And the greatest gift wasn't placed under the tree. It was a placed upon the tree for you and me, so that we could see that we could be, made free, to be made right with God through Jesus Christ our Lord.

Bibles Back In Schools
By Samantha Wilezol

We don't doubt history books in school. As a matter of fact, we see to not repeat others' mistakes, and how wars caused more wars. Humans weren't successful. Columbus sailed the sea and thought the earth was flat, but went out in faith. Lincoln signed the proclamation. We believe in history books, so don't doubt God. The history books disappoint, but God's Word never disappoints; there's artifacts from history books, and paintings, and same with the Bible in Jesus. We believe the events in history books, though we didn't see the events happen, and even though no artifacts are not in front of us or the person. We learn of Columbus and Lincoln, in public schools and religious schools.

What leaders thought was the right way to lead to fix everything and make everyone happy didn't work. God's Word, the instruction manual of how to live life, never disappoints. It doesn't always make sense, but it never disappoints.

Volcanoes are hard to believe that they are true in books, but we see that they are, as an example.

Jesus Is A Living Fact, That Wants To Be Real In Your Life, Not A Made Up Idea
By Samantha Wilezol

Did you know the Bible points to all of life? See John 1:1 in the Amplified Version. Jesus is a fact to believe in that makes him real in our lives through believing in faith, so can be brought back to schools.

Abide In
By Samantha Wilezol

I used to work with the president's wife's sister at a coffee shop in Ocean City, New Jersey. I got the revelation that to "Abide in" (God) sounds like the president's last name.

A Washing for Washington (D.C.), And Beyond!
By Samantha Wilezol

Flying in a plane sounded out of the ordinary, but the Wright brothers tried to in faith, in which I believe my grandfather is related to them. Some may not know if the Bible can change their life but they try it anyway. History books are old or not popular, but are still studied, so why is the Bible taken out? Some may think the Bible is biased, but Jesus is true, Jesus is the Word!

It makes sense why kids were more well-behaved, and the world more in order when Bibles were allowed in school. The basis of God made our states united, but what caused division and prejudice and sin? (Greed and anger). Be transformed by the renewing of her mind, the Bible shares. A change in root yields changing in fruit; we can't change our kids' behavior or our own or the world, because we all have an inner problem of sin that only God can fix, proof Jesus is real. The Bible was able to address that problem, so why would anyone make up a problem of the world?

God helped me to propose for no more letters or grades because we don't have to earn our way towards God. Likewise, we don't have to earn approval from teachers or parents through our works.

History Of Princesses Should Be Taught In Schools
By Samantha Wilezol

Seeing that princesses are real and have really existed in the United States helps to reinforce that living out the seven fruits of the spirit are not going out of style. Many fictional princesses showed those characteristics, but real princesses have too. Let's encourage the next generation of young girls to be informed of real princesses that existed in the country so that when they get older, they may not think that showing respect and loyalty are not fictional things, and so that they may be open to the true concept of being loyal in Christ Jesus, believing in God and who they are and Jesus when they get older.

May the love and joy that enters into little girls' hearts who
look to Princess Ariel relate to the love and joy of
Princess Grace Kelly who lived in New Jersey who shared love and joy through her acting.

May the peace and patience of Princess Jasmine relate to Princess Lisa
Halaby of New Jersey who shared those qualities through her work in Urban
Planning and encouraging women in America to have the same qualities.

May the kindness and goodness of princess Snow White relate to
Princess Marie-Chantal Miller of N.Y. who shared those qualities
through finding her own company in a clothing brand for kids.

May the faithfulness, gentleness, and self-control of Cinderella relate to Princess Sarah
Butler of Texas who portrayed those same qualities through supporting the "White Ribbon
Alliance for Safe Motherhood", and the "Women's Rights Division at Human Rights Watch".

May the qualities of princesses that stem from the seven fruits of the spirit
not be viewed as mundane from fictional cartoon princess characters, but be
continued in women today through real U.S. princesses who showed those same
qualities. May being royalty in Christ Jesus not be a foreign concept, but rather
believed at a young age so adults may be open to receiving King Jesus.

(Information learned through verbal sharings from museums)

No More College Debt
By Samantha Wilezol

It's interesting how many people go to college to try to form their own identity. They may spend their whole lives paying off the debt and they may feel guilt of having tried to form their own identity, and from spending their whole lives trying to pay that back.

What if I told you someone paid your debt for you and that your identity is found in someone alone?

And that Jesus paid your debt for you at the cross, so that your identity doesn't have to be defined in what you do but rather who you are in Him.

So we can get out of this net of debt,
Be freed from this sticky glue of what we do,
And raise the bar
To see who we are
In Christ alone.

So stop stressing about your major, trying to get any degree, because to live is Christ and to die is gain!

**Side note: A lady I worked with is related to the president who advocated for forgiveness from loans of students!

No More Letters Or Grades In Schools
By Samantha Wilezol

Your conduct and what you verbalize is stemmed from, well, what you think.

It makes sense why there was a difference in our kids' behavior when their thought process came from reading the Bible in the schools. That was five out of seven days a week of correct nurturing of the mind influencing their first nature as adults, that time in age being the critical years of forming first nature in someone's mind.

Once again, many may wonder why they can't change their kids' or own behavior, and it's because we all have an internal issue and problem that only God can fix. Sin. That's why Jesus had to come.

I would like to advocate to bring Bibles and Jesus back into the school system because I think our founding fathers knew something we didn't know, that when this nation was founded as a nation under God and when Bibles were allowed in the school system, kids' behavior in general was more respectful, and society seemed more in order.

Also, kids' thought process of if they earned approval from my parents or teachers can stem into wrongly thinking if they can *earn* approval from God. Having grades and letters within grades in the school system that maybe unknowingly causing this wrong thought process stated above could most likely sadly have them be skeptical of thinking that we have to earn approval from God. No, we are made right with him through His Grace.

Considering SAT scores are not mandatory for college entrances, I would like to advocate for letter grades not existing in the school system anymore; But rather, the kid simply passes the class or is asked to get a week or two of extra help before being able to pass into the next. Or, each letter representing something positive in the grade system.

My grandfather, Ronald Reit, showed me that I have rights (reit)!

Link to me speaking on these in Washington D.C and at City Council meetings, all for Jesus' glory, including other original content by Samantha Wilezol, in this book protected through "Westbow Press": https://docs.google.com/document/d/1Avw-XS9 PZwD5zBb5UH3pUfRsl9aWGyuXcmnXXA_ykcA/edit

It can be easy for some to say "I was born this way", but Jesus explains how you must be born again!

Some may wonder, "Why does sin feel so "good"?" It's because your *fleshly* part of your body sadly isn't concerned that your spirit is going with you, to heaven. But as Christ followers, that's why we can further share of his love!

A pastor is called a "past-or" because they preach of how our past has been redeemed!

Some may say "life feels so long, so I might as well live for the moment / stress of making something HUGE for myself", but Christ followers say "life is so short compared to eternity, I might as well lose it to further eternity." After all, how much of your reality is invested into eternity?

College fraternity, brothers and sisters validate you for what you do but brothers and sisters in Christ reassure you of who you are in Christ and who he is alone.

Living by faith, is like using a magnifying glass.

The Sticks Analogy
By Samantha Wilezol

The first humans on earth noticed two sticks and thought that they looked boring and thought they didn't have any power, but when they rubbed them together for long enough, they created a spark that could start a fire for survival, sticks that create paper.

Likewise, when a skeptic looks at the paper pages of the Bible, they may think it looks "boring" or outdated, but when you rub the paper pages together so to speak, (or turn from one page to the next), to give it a chance, you'll see it can create a spark in your heart.

Similar to how lint also starts a fire, "lint" sounds like "lent", a Biblical term.

Wondering
By Samantha Wilezol

For people who ask, "If the Bible is true?", what is the basis they are asking off of? Do they feel true on the inside? Because even the highest CEO of a business who is trying to prove something can feel untrue on the inside, and may think on being told he wasn't good enough when he was five years old before his head hitting the pillow at night.

An Artistic Approach To Reach Teenagers
referring to posting on your story online and friending people online:
Text From The Text By Samantha Wilezol

God posts on his story about you all the time, on the circle story icon, that is in the shape of the constant, whole, infinite circle of God's agape love, it's just you haven't clicked on it yet. He already friended you, you just have to friend him back. There was a glitch (sin) (us), so a landline had to come, for jeez, us! Wait, that sounds like someone. Jesus!

The Message Behind The Risen Cross
By Samantha Wilezol

A. All of direction points to the risen cross of Jesus
B. The risen cross of Jesus points to His love for you
C. The risen cross of Jesus wants to hug you and relate with you
D. As Christ followers, we can live in upward love to him an outward serving towards others in His love!

Go to the Shore of a Bank
By Samantha Wilezol

Go to the shore of a bank, to be assured of your infinite worth. The source is from the sand that God made. Not even a scientist knows the number of grains of sand, so it is to trust not tangibly understand. Bend down, and you might find a Sandollar. The source is from that of infinite, like how God's thoughts towards us are as infinite as the grains of sand on the seashore.

(All Writings Below and Throughout by Samantha Wilezol)

When you feel insecure, you're actually in secure.

Cross on food labels can be related to Jesus in deeper meaning, as an analogy.

Saturn has a ring around it, pointing to the word "hupamome", meaning to stand under (to understand)!

The one born in the year of Four points to the one who forgave you, who was foretold, and who foretold your existence, and who points to forever. He said he was the chosen one "b4" anyone else: King Jesus!- By Samantha Wilezol

The first bibliography came from the Biblia. We don't doubt other biographies, so don't doubt this one, of King Jesus!

Hupomone means to stand under. When elaborated on, to understand (stand under to understand)! -Samantha Wilezol

By Samantha Wilezol
Dios sounds like diez

10 means wholeness (10 fingers). God is wholeness, like the circle of the planets pointing to wholeness!

love: Ojos to see(ve)

Proof that God is love
By Samantha Wilezol

When you say *love*, it sounds like "of".
"Of" in Spanish is "de". Love is of us. So who is of us?
Di in Spanish means "gave".
Os in Spanish means "you".
Dios points to the one who "gave you" a second chance!

Side note: Pillars of Creation is interesting.

Love points to God
By Samantha Wilezol

"Amor" means "love" in Spanish.
"Amor" broken down means "to more" (a more).
"Mas", or "more", is in "Christmas"
Love points to Christ, and all of mass points to Christ!

Palabra from the Palabora: The Message for "U"
By Samantha Wilezol

On a coordinate plane, in this illustration, picture "time" on the Y axis.
Time was counting down, leading to the year of when
Jesus was born (see the point on the Y axis).
Time is counting up to when he will return, because time
was counting down to when he would come.
Pt 2: Problema since the Placenta
By Samantha Wilezol
We were all born into sin, also known as "without", that can be represented as zero.
After God sent the great flood during the Noah And The Ark occurrence,
there was an intersection point (see where the two parabolas meet),
at the year of 33, representing Jesus' 33 years on the earth.
In math, the point where two parabolas meet is called the "origin", so this is a cool,
visual way to see how indeed, Jesus is the origin of all life and for the universe!
Analogies in math can be helpful to use to help understand
"Math"ew, a supplement to understanding.

*Note to readers: Link to pictures in this book, including cover picture, below for a bigger/clearer view of them, including original haikus by Samantha Wilezol, too: https://docs.google.com/document/d/1uwGfeRIX40TbLk4MmYllp_wnmYllLWl5PAhRV5vuC-A/edit?usp=sharing

Science is taught in schools though a fake religion "Scientology" exists.

Jesus should legally be taught in schools because He is a living fact, and is the only true belief! ****

Thank you for reading this book by Samantha Wilezol, who loves Jesus Christ, and who had the opportunity to graduate from Stockton University in Galloway, N.J.! God bless you all! Jesus is King! * Message for the world: John 3:16 ; Romans 10:9 ; Matthew 16:24-25

This is an original picture from Samantha Wilezol as well,
protected in this book through "Westbow Press"!

The alteration of thought comes through maintaining our roots in Jesus Christ's love!

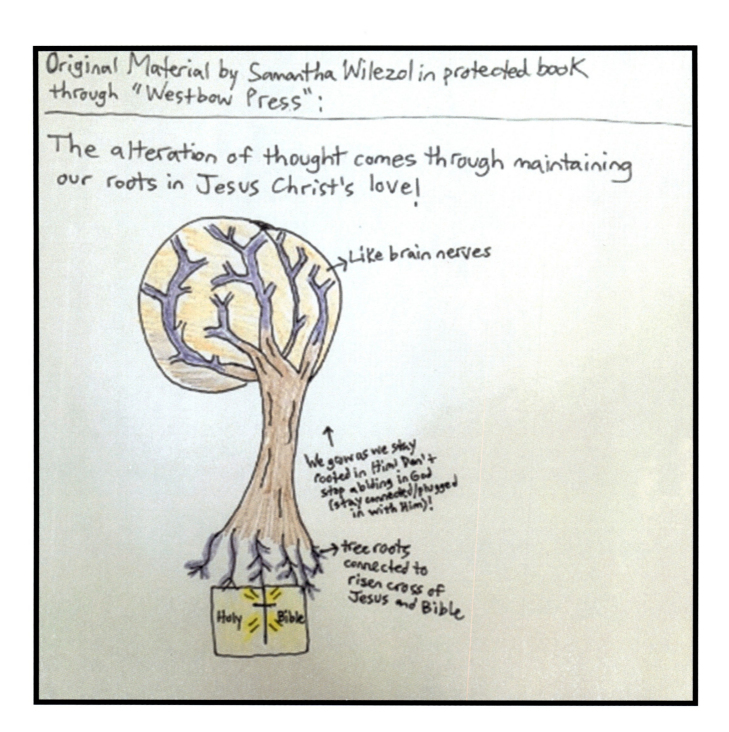

Like brain nerves

We grow as we stay rooted in Him! Don't stop abiding in God (stay connected/plugged in with Him)!

tree roots connected to risen cross of Jesus and Bible

Holy Bible

Original Material by Samantha Wilezol, in book protected through "Westpress Bow":

What → hat → ✝hat

Where → here → ✝here

When → hen → ✝hen

. . . .

✳ When we exchange our "shoulder shrug" questions about life with looking to the risen cross of Jesus, we can see life through the awesome lense of faith!

-Samantha Wilezol

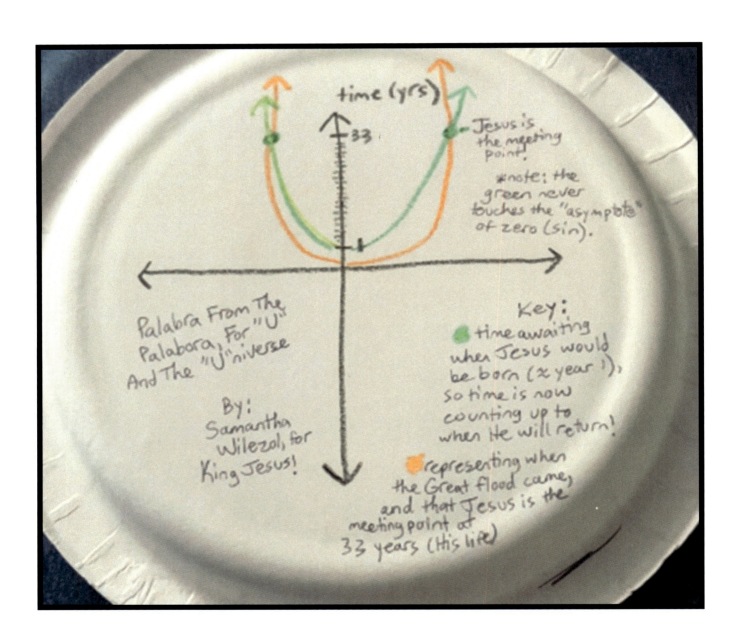

Original material by Samantha Wilczol,
on my protected book through "Westbow Press"

Laminin → ☨ → <mark>Jesus</mark>

<mark>B.C and A.C</mark> → Christ

<mark>Four things to live</mark> → Jesus → Jesus, the Bread, Light, Water, & Breath of all life

(Air, water, food, and sunlight)

John 8:35
John 20: 21-22
John 7:37-39
John 8:12

John 1:1

"In the <mark>beginning</mark> [before all time] was the

Word <mark>(Christ)</mark>, and the Word was with God, and the

Word was God Himself"

And so my friends, the Uni-Verse for the Universe is John 3:16, that "For God so loved the world, that he gave his only Son, that whoever believes in him should not perish but have eternal life".

Putting that into action, "If you declare with your mouth, "Jesus is Lord," and believe in your heart that God raised him from the dead, you will be saved"(Romans 10:9). Remember, friends, that the message from God of the Universe (Un-I-ver-se) is "One I to see, He (Jesus).

God bless you all, and thank you for journeying with me in "The Uni Verse for the Universe"! **Un-** Be *und*one (surrendered) to be shown the unknown, who wants to make Himself known to you, **I-** The Great I Am (God)- **Ver-** Believing is seeing (Jesus) ; **Se-** The words "love" and "Dios" looked at more closely, broken down, point to how God is a He (of the Trinity, who came to earth in flesh form, Jesus). - Samantha Wilezol

Samantha Wilezol of South Jersey loves Jesus Christ and went to college at Stockton University in South Jersey! Her ministry name "Reit, His Will Is All (Wil-ez-ol)" for Jesus aspires to have an addendum name added to it, so keep your eye out! Follow her online @samanthawilezol

Author Biography:

Samantha Wilezol has earned her B.S. from Stockton University in Galloway, New Jersey, and is the founder of the "Reit, His Will Is All (Wil-ez-ol)" International Ministry, "Reit" after her Grandpa who was a pilot (ministry name subject to change)! For updates, see @samanthawilezol and @ reit_his_will_is_all_intl

One of Samantha Wilezol's great relatives through ancestry is Nobel Peace Prize winner Elie Wilezol, as she is giving recognition of him through the book. She also wrote two books so far from at the age of just 22, and inspirationally speaks. Her inspiration is her faith. Additionally, she is fluent in Spanish, and worked with individuals out of D.C. in Ocean City, New Jersey, to help advocate for change, beginning at a heart level.

Also, she has co-spoken with a national apologetist and was on the "Great American Speak Off" show. In addition, she is an illustrator, has painted the cover for this book, and also published a book at just five years old. Her faith inspires her daily.

Printed in the United States
by Baker & Taylor Publisher Services